HIGLEY

HIGLEY

A Story of Bob Higley, His short life of Sacrifice for his country, love for his wife and how HIS LEGACY CREATED GREAT JOY FOR SO MANY

JAMES GRABAU

Library of Congress Control Number:		2020912560
ISBN:	Hardcover	978-1-9845-8714-5
	Softcover	978-1-9845-8713-8
	eBook	978-1-9845-8712-1

Print information available on the last page.

Rev. date: 07/17/2020

To order additional copies of this book, contact:
Xlibris
1-888-795-4274
www.Xlibris.com
Orders@Xlibris.com
810325

This is a story of Bob Higley, his short life of sacrifice
for his country, love for his wife, and how

HIS LEGACY CREATED GREAT JOY FOR SO MANY.

DEDICATION

I would like to Dedicate this book to Virginia (Ginny) Adam Higley Pennington. I could not have written the book *Higley* without all the care and painstaking scrap books, letters. and history that Ginny kept of Bob's Navy Service and their life during World War II. Virginia, as I knew her, passed away at the age of 92 on January 15, 2015. She reared five children, Sherry, Nancy, Jimmy, Johnny and Gail. I found these momentos in her attic and asked permission to take them to my home for keepsakes. I copied all of the material and sent originals to Sherry her eldest daughter. I divided Bob's medals and gave half to Sherry and had the others framed for Nancy.

I would also like to dedicate this book to Virginia's first daughter Sherry Higley Wasserburger, who passed away on April 27, 2018 at the age of seventy-five in San Diego, California. Sherry is very much missed by her family and those who knew her.

Finally I dedicate this book to the memory of Bob Higley, and others like him, who gave of himself to preserve our freedom, so that we may enjoy every day we live in this great country.

James Grabau

PROLOGUE

On the cover of *Higley*, is a hand-colored (as was the fashion of the 1920's), black and white photograph of young Robert (Bob) Harrison Higley, dressed in a child's sailor suit. This portrait, taken when young Higley was four or five years old, foretold a future he was destined to live.

Bob was born in the Ancon Canal Zone of Panama, on June 8,1917, three months after the United States entered World War I. The war known at the time as "the war to end all wars."

Bob grew up in Kansas City, Missouri, to join what we now call the Greatest Generation, that group of individuals, especially the young men who would fight in World War II, and were born between 1901 and 1924. As he grew-up, he felt indestructible, like all of us do when we are young, and life seemed as if it would last forever.

This, then, is the story of Bob Higley: his love for the woman he married during the early days of World War II, for the challenges posed by war that he faced, and his bravery in meeting those challenges. He never got to see his family grow up. He was lost on a bombing mission in the Pacific when his first daughter was a few months old, although he did get to see her; he never saw his younger daughter who was born after his disappearance.

War is counter productive. Besides the great loss of life and productivity it turns peoples' lives upside down. People have dreams and goals, but war has no consideration for them. We are thankful for people like Bob Higley who set aside their future plans to answer the call to help preserve the world's freedom and that of the United States. We should enjoy the freedom for which they fought so hard and never forget those who gave their lives to preserve it. I wanted to tell Bob's story: it is not only the story of a brave man and equally brave wife but also because their story comprises the heritage of the daughter who grew up to marry me. I can't imagine my life without my last fifty some years with Bob's and Ginny's second daughter, Nancy.

LIFE IN THE FORTIES

To understand Bob's story, we first need to look back a little bit, to see what the forties were like. The following was taken from *The Readers Digest*, A Sentimental Journey, "AMERICA IN THE 40's".

During this period America changed more rapidly than any other period in our history. In ten years the country will go from a sleeping giant to a super power. From the simplicity of an agricultural industrial age to the complexities of the atomic age. It will go from a country whose military used rifles made in 1917 to the strongest nation the world has ever seen. In 1940, America was still a nation of small towns, general stores, picket fences. and front porch swings. Just as small towns dominated the American landscape, so too small-town life defined the American character. In the 40's, life was made up of box lunches at church socials, hand-cranked phones and party lines, iceboxes, radios, clothespins, pincushions, 7 o'clock breakfasts with griddle cakes, bacon, eggs, and coffee. Most women still sewed. Children wizzed down neighborhood streets on roller skates and ate double-dip ice cream cones. A young man in the 1940's might be seen walking down the street with a pack of Pall Malls in his pocket, Vitalis in his hair, penny loafers, a sport coat with the shirt collar spread over it so he was all shoulders and shoes walking into the drugstore whistling "FOOLS RUSH IN," A young girl might be wearing sharp little bobby socks, sweater and pearls, or an apron dress, drinking a coke as she sat in the drug store. The soda jerk would think all the girls had a crush on him, his white paper hat cocked to one side. A car cost about $700, and gas was 12 cents a gallon. At the start of the decade most Americans did not own a car and couldn't even drive. As the country emerged from The Great Depression, most Americans were cautiously optimistic about the future. Another cause for American optimism in 1940 was the completion of Rockefeller Center.

It was the most ambitious privately funded building project that had been started after the onset of the Great Depression. American industry was developing at a rapid pace. This was driven by events occurring in Europe that spring. With the Nazi invasion of Denmark and Norway the illusion was shattered that the European war could be a limited one.

President Roosevelt requested that congress double its appropriations for both the Army and the Navy. He also proposed that the production of military aircraft be increased from 12,000 to 50,000 that year. Congress appropriated $2.1 billion for national defense, five times the amount appropriated in 1939. America had indeed become the "Arsenal of Democracy." As far as many people were concerned we were already in the war up to our elbows. There was a tremendous increase in air travel in 1940 and 1941. Most of which was domestic, and much of it related to the booming defense industry. Americans who couldn't afford air travel would turn to sports for diversion. The last summer before the war, was a golden age for sports. Joe DiMaggio and Ted Williams shared center stage. In 1942 baseball was truly the national pastime as it never had been before and probably will never be again. The crowds at the 1941 World Series between the Yankees and the Dodgers were more raucous and more high-spirited than usual. All manner of celebrities were on hand. President Roosevelt took a break and listened to the entire game on the radio. The Yanks won 3-2. It was as if everyone felt that the next World Series would be played in a different and darker world. And they were right! It was a much simpler world in the early 1940's. Chattanooga Choo Choo by Glen Miller was a hit song. Ronald Reagan starred in a movie called" International Squadron" produced by Warner Brothers. Robert Allen Zimmerman was born, who later changed his name to

Bob Dylan. Others born to become famous included Faye Dunaway, Neil Diamond, Ann-Margret, Chubby Checker; and Jesse Jackson. (My sister Emily was also born in 1941.) The average income was $1,777.00. A new house was $4075.00 and average rent was $32.00 per month. A first class postage stamp cost 3 cents and a movie ticket was 30 cents. Sugar sold for 59 cents for ten pounds. Bread was 8 cents per loaf and eggs 20 cents a dozen. On Sunday, December 7,1941, that idyllic world was shattered. A young man might have been out back trying to start his jalopy, when he heard his mother holler, and that meant "right now!", come inside! She's not just listening to the radio, it's like she's watching it. He hears "Japanese" and "Pearl Harbor. On that day, a foreign military force, had attacked US soil for the first time in more than 125 years. The United States and the world changed forever that day.

YOUNG BOB HIGLEY

Robert Harrison Higley was born June 8, 1917 in Ancon, Canal Zone, to Harrison and Mayme Higley. The family moved to Kansas City when Bob was very young, living at 7915 Ward Parkway. Bob grew up in a typical Midwestern family with one younger sister, Virginia. Bob was not a large boy and grew to about five foot eleven inches and one hundred sixty pounds. He learned to play tennis and golf. He was a nice looking young man of slight build with dark hair and a pleasant personality. Bob graduated from Westport High School in 1935. After high school, Bob enrolled in a community college in Kansas City and received his two year degree in 1937. While still in school, Bob had joined the Army National Guard in 1934, and had worked at part time jobs during the Depression. President Roosevelt had established the "New Deal", in 1933 to help stimulate the US economy, but money was still very tight. Bob lived with his parents to save money and also worked part-time to help them out with finances.

Mayme Higley and Bob

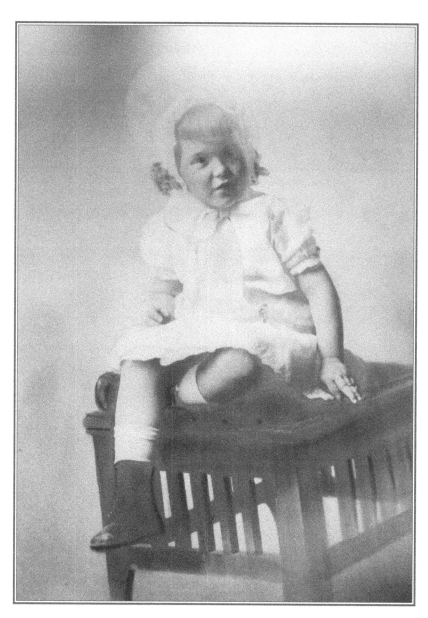

Bob's younger sister Virginia Higley

Bob in straw hat   Young Bob Higley

Bob's High School Graduation Picture

YOUNG VIRGINIA ADAM

Virginia Ruth Adam was born June 13, 1922 to James McIntosh Adam and Ruth Couffer Adam in Oak Park, Illinois. When the Great Depression hit in 1929 the Adam family moved in with the Couffer family to save money. The Adam family lived in the upstairs of the home, and the Couffer family lived in the lower level of the home. The Couffer family consisted of Bob, Ruth's brother, his wife Fran, and their children Jane and Bobby. The Adam family included James, Ruth, Virginia and Jean. It was often said that when the families separated there were many tears shed.

Virginia lived in Oak Park until she was ten years old and then the family moved to Kansas City, Missouri. She had a younger sister named Jean. Virginia, or as her friends called her, "Ginny", was schooled in Kansas City and graduated from Southwest High School in 1940.

Ginny and her cousin, Jane, enrolled at Beloit College in Beloit, Wisconsin, in the fall of 1940. They both pledged Pi Beta Phi Sorority.

Young Virginia Adam

Virginia and Jean Adam

Virginia (Ginny) with friends at Beloit College, Beloit Wisconsin

MILITARY FLIGHT TRAINING

In 1940, Bob switched from the Army National Guard to the Navy Air Corps Reserve. He was sent to Pensacola, Florida, for flight training, where he started January 21,1941. He was later transferred to Miami, Florida, on June 23,1941. He became an Official Naval Aviator July 10, 1941. His first orders were to Fleet Air Detachment, Naval Air Station, Norfolk, Virginia, for temporary duty involving flying under training. Reporting on August 24, 1941, he accepted an appointment and executed his oath of office as Lieutenant (Junior Grade) to rank from June 15,1942.

Training for flyers usually began with bi-planes in the twenties and thirties at Pensacola, Florida. It quickly graduated to more sophisticated planes as the student flyers progressed. Before the Japanese attack on Pearl Harbor, the Navy had only one flight school and about 100 student entries per month. This number soon increased to three main stations with more than 800 students per month. Pensacola, the original, now had 300 per month, Jacksonville, Florida, 200, and Corpus Christi, Texas, 300. At the start of the United States entrance to World War II there were 4,300 naval aviators (including Marines) on the rolls and 2,700 students under training.

Rear Admiral John H. Towers, Chief of the Bureau of Aeronautics was most concerned with naval air expansion. He was the number one senior pilot by historical fact, not by virtue of his present rank. Even before the U.S. entered the war, he had begun to oversee the development of better and more advanced planes taking place.

This article, entitled, "Pilots and Planes Are Made For Job," I found in Ginny's scrapbook, describes the training dive bombers and torpedo bombers received. Future dive bombers come to the Advanced Carrier Training Groups from the vast Navy Air Schools of Pensacola, Jacksonville and Corpus Christi. When they arrive they are commissioned officers, with their gold Navy wings and a good background in flying. When they leave, they are as integral a part of an SBD as its control stick or telescope sight. This transformation is achieved by instructors who are crack dive bombers, most of whom have proved their worth at the Gilbert Islands, the Coral Sea or Midway. The first thing the students are taught is that dive bombing is a precise science, governed by the laws of gravity and the speed of the wind. They are shown that in the perfect dive from 10,000 feet, at an angle approximating 75 degrees, if the plane is not skidding to the right or lefthand if the wind estimation is accurate, a bomb released at 2500 ft. will infallibly hit its target. It takes long patient weeks to make students act as an agent of this law. The sensations of diving are so alien to the human system that it requires practice to become accustomed to them. And in the few seconds of a dive, pilots cannot rely solely on instruments to show them they are diving correctly. That is a matter of physical feeling and a well developed sense of how the plane is responding. These the pilot must learn for himself. The pilot learns in the plane he will use in real dive-bombing attacks. It was built for this express purpose, with wide diving breaks on the wings, reinforcement to stand the rigors of dives, a split-second bomb release and displacing gear to kick the falling bomb away from the propeller. Together, the planes and pilots make an unbeatable team.

Training can be almost as dangerous as flying into battle. More than 15,000 pilots died while training during WWII. The reason for this is not just one thing but many. Even though the men were prequalified for flight school they could still make mistakes while taking off, flying, or landing. Sometimes the planes themselves failed and the result a crash, not due to pilot error or even mechanical error. Weather conditions also caused problems for the aircraft and its pilot.

The fate of Iowa flier Nile Kinnick is a case in point. Kinnick lost his life during a training mission in Venezuela. Nile Kinnick was a half back for the University of Iowa in the late 1930's. He won the Heisman Trophy in 1939 after being voted the best college football player in the nation that year. He also was named the Big Ten MVP, All American, Associated Press Athlete of the Year, Walter Camp Trophy Winner that same year. In his Heisman acceptance speech, which is still quoted today, he gave credit to his teammates as well as those fighting in Europe against the Germans. He was very concerned about the war even before the United States had entered it.

Kinnick graduated third in his class and decided to enter the university's law school rather than accepting the National Football League's offer to play pro-football. He had been offered a large sum of money to play pro-football for the Brooklyn Dodgers, not to be confused with the baseball team of the same name. The Brooklyn Dodgers had played in the National Football League (NFL) from

1930 to 1943 and in 1944 as the Brooklyn Tigers. The team played its home games at Ebbets Field, the same field where the baseball team of the same name played. Kinnick dropped out of Law School after one year to join the Naval Air Force Reserve. It was a courageous decision from an incredible human being. His reason was simple: it was the right thing to do. He wrote," There is no reason in the world why we shouldn't fight for the preservation of a chance to live freely, no reason why we shouldn't suffer to uphold that which we want to endure. May God give me the courage to do my duty and not falter… Every man that I have admired in history has willingly and courageously served in his country's armed forces in times of danger. It is not only a duty but an honor to follow their example the best I know how. May God give me the courage and ability to so conduct myself in every situation that my country, my family, and my friends will be proud of me."

Once enlisted, Kinnick began training to be a fighter pilot. It was something he seemed both to enjoy and feel a great sense of duty in doing. In a letter to his parents less than two years into his service, Kinnick wrote, "The task which lies ahead is adventure as well as duty, and I am anxious to get at it. I feel better in mind and body than I have for ten years and am quite certain I can meet the foe confident and unafraid. I have set the Lord always before me, because he is my right hand. I shall not be moved. Truly, we have shared to the full life, love, and laughter. Comforted in the knowledge that your faith and courage will never falter, no matter the outcome, I bid you au revoir."

A few weeks later, Nile Kinnick was dead. On June 3, 1943, Kinnick departed the USS *Lexington* on a routine training mission off the coast of Venezuela. In the midst of his flight, his Grumman F4F Wildcat began leaking oil. Eventually, it went dry and Kinnick was caught too far from the coast and too far from his aircraft carrier to make a safe landing. He followed procedure, attempting a water landing, but did not survive. His body was never recovered. He was 24 years old.

Nile Kinnick is remembered as an Iowa and American hero. He was a tremendous football player, a great student, and even better person.(In 1972, the stadium at the University of Iowa was renamed in his honor, and in 2007, the school unveiled a statue of Kinnick near the stadium's main entrance.) He gave up his hopes and aspirations to serve his country and he gave his life doing so. In that regard he shared a lot of similarities with Bob Higley. They both had joined the Navy Reserve after college. Both had gone through training at Pensacola, received their wings and were assigned to an aircraft carrier. Both loved their country and had a strong faith in God. War and the preparation for war had changed their lives as well as those of others, even as it does today.

Nile Kinnick Training to be a Fighter pilot

To give you a time line of Bob's life in the service these dates are documented:

Page one of Navy Department Officer Service Summary

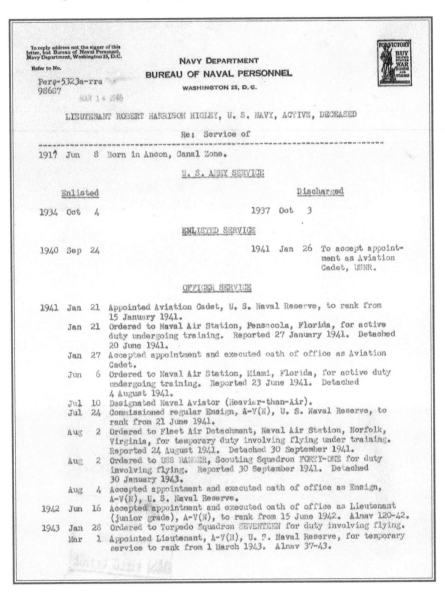

Refer to No.

Pers-5323a-rra
98687

MAR 14 1946

NAVY DEPARTMENT
BUREAU OF NAVAL PERSONNEL
WASHINGTON 25, D.C.

LIEUTENANT ROBERT HARRISON HIGLEY, U. S. NAVY, ACTIVE, DECEASED

Re: Service of

1917 Jun 8 Born in Ancon, Canal Zone.

U. S. ARMY SERVICE

Enlisted	Discharged
1934 Oct 4	1937 Oct 3

ENLISTED SERVICE

1940 Sep 24	1941 Jan 26 To accept appointment as Aviation Cadet, USNR.

OFFICER SERVICE

1941 Jan 21 Appointed Aviation Cadet, U. S. Naval Reserve, to rank from 15 January 1941.

Jan 21 Ordered to Naval Air Station, Pensacola, Florida, for active duty undergoing training. Reported 27 January 1941. Detached 20 June 1941.

Jan 27 Accepted appointment and executed oath of office as Aviation Cadet.

Jun 6 Ordered to Naval Air Station, Miami, Florida, for active duty undergoing training. Reported 23 June 1941. Detached 4 August 1941.

Jul 10 Designated Naval Aviator (Heavier-than-Air).

Jul 24 Commissioned regular Ensign, A-V(N), U. S. Naval Reserve, to rank from 21 June 1941.

Aug 2 Ordered to Fleet Air Detachment, Naval Air Station, Norfolk, Virginia, for temporary duty involving flying under training. Reported 24 August 1941. Detached 30 September 1941.

Aug 2 Ordered to USS RANGER, Scouting Squadron FORTY-ONE for duty involving flying. Reported 30 September 1941. Detached 30 January 1943.

Aug 4 Accepted appointment and executed oath of office as Ensign, A-V(N), U. S. Naval Reserve.

1942 Jun 16 Accepted appointment and executed oath of office as Lieutenant (junior grade), A-V(N), to rank from 15 June 1942. Alnav 120-42.

1943 Jan 28 Ordered to Torpedo Squadron SEVENTEEN for duty involving flying.

Mar 1 Appointed Lieutenant, A-V(N), U. S. Naval Reserve, for temporary service to rank from 1 March 1943. Alnav 37-43.

Early Service Career Record

Bob Higley Navy Pilot

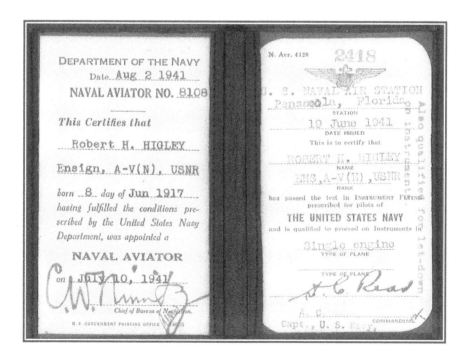

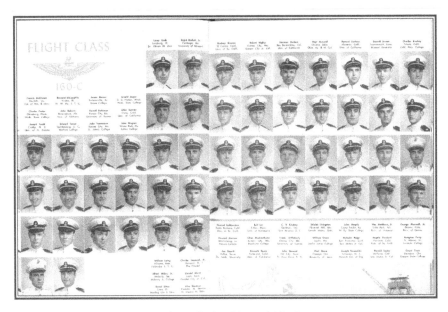

Bob's Flight Class 160-C

Ensign Higley Graduation Photo

ROMANCE

Bob Higley's family home at 7915 Ward Parkway was not too far from where the Adam family lived at 1288 West 71st Terrace. Bob met Ginny's father on a near by golf course not far from where they both lived and they would play occasionally. James Adam, Ginny's father became fond of Bob and invited him to dinner to meet his family. Bob no doubt must have noticed that the Adam daughters's were very pretty. He asked Ginny to go out with him and they started dating.

The romance between Ginny and Bob progressed rapidly as they had little time together because of Bob's training as well as Ginny's first year of college. Bob was five years older than Ginny and, I think, operated on a different timetable than Ginny. With war looming many couples' courtships were brief.

They fell in love and Bob popped the question and Ginny said yes. I do not know the details, if Bob asked Ginny's father for her hand, as was the custom back then, but her parents must have approved because they threw a big engagement party at their home for 100 guests. I did see a note in Ginny's scrap book that indicated the date she accepted was August 20, 1941. Her scrap book is also filled with congratulation cards from all of her friends. Bob wore his Navy Dress Uniform and notes in Ginny's scrap book said it was a big social success.

Ensign Higley's first duty assignment was to the naval base in Norfolk, Virginia. He was to be a Navy flier with the scouting squadron # 41 aboard the carrier *USS Ranger*

The *Ranger* was the first Aircraft Carrier that was designed for that use and not a converted ship. The *USS Ranger* was authorized February 13, 1929. Her keel was laid September 26, 1931 by Newport News Shipbuilding and Dry Dock Company, Newport, News, Virginia. She was launched February 25, 1933, and commissioned June 4, 1934. The ship was equipped to operate 75 modern aircraft, and armed with six 40mm quadruple mounts and forty-six 20mm mounts. She was one of the early carriers, also referred to as flattops, to pass through the Panama Canal on the way to the Pacific in early 1939. John S. McCain Sr. was Captain of the *USS Ranger* from 1937 to 1939.

FLATTOP RIDES THE MISSISSIPPI—The Ranger, first full-sized American aircraft carrier ever to enter the Mississippi river, is shown heading upstream for New Orleans. Late esterday the Ranger, accompanied by the battleship Mississippi, docked at New Orleans—(Wirephoto).

The Ranger Carrier

Bob and Ginny had planned to marry after the required year Bob had to serve in the Navy. Bob was now flying scout missions from the *U.S.S, Ranger.* The ship operated with both the Atlantic and Pacific Fleet, where she performed routine training functions and participated in routine battle maneuvers. On December 7, 1941 she arrived at the Naval Operations Base, Norfolk, Virginia, having just completed a voyage to the southeast Atlantic as an escort to a British troop convoy. Meanwhile a rather significant event happened at Pearl Harbor, Hawaii. Most Americans, no doubt had thought we would have to enter the war sometime, but no one thought it would be by Japanese attack.

The United States was caught totally off guard. No other event could have been a more painful and shocking "wake up call"! There may have been some preliminary planning for the United States' eventual entry into the war, but suddenly it had taken on an urgent reality.

At 12:30 p.m. on December 8, 1941 President Franklin Roosevelt requested Congress to pass a declaration of war against Japan, which it did at 1:10 p.m. Roosevelt signed the declaration at 4:10 that afternoon. Declarations of war against Germany and Italy followed two days later. when we would enter the war, but now it had become a reality! Headlines in papers across the United States read on Monday morning:

HEADLINE FROM DES MOINES REGISTER UNITED STATES AT WAR JAPS BOMB OUR BASES

After Pearl Harbor's attack there was a huge rush of men enlisting in all branches of the armed service to fight for our country. This truly was a real World War that affected everyone from Europe to the South Pacific.

I think Ginny must have wondered how the war would affect her plans of marriage and her future with Bob? She knew about military service, as her dad, James Adam, was a Captan in the Marine Corps. She wasn't being selfish, and was well aware of Bob's responsibility for his country, but was only human to wonder what the future would hold.

Like most Americans, Ginny scanned the newspapers and listened to the radio broadcast. She was very observant and read an article in the paper that said the following: (Reserve Pilots May Wed) found in the Kansas City Star (the headline) Washington, January 21,1942- Romance got a break from the Navy today. Secretary Knox has approved a new regulation permitting aviators of the Navy and Marine Corps reserves to marry immediately after completing their flight training. She even had this newspaper clipping in her scrap book.

The statement that Japan had woken a sleeping giant was very true. Pearl Harbor was a very painful lesson but it taught us that we could no longer depend on the oceans to isolate us from the rest of the world. The Ranger was not in the war right away. She was sent to Bermuda until March 13, 1942 making several routine training cruises. She proceeded from Bermuda, arriving in Norfolk, Virginia March 19,1942 where she was to undergo a 16 day period in the Norfolk Navy Yard for war refurbishing. The Ranger was the largest carrier in the Atlantic Fleet.

WEDDING BELLS 1942

Because War had been declared, and the regulations had been changed, both Bob and Ginny thought it was their best chance to marry. Bob could take some leave time, as the *Ranger* was being gone through to make it battle ready. The wedding was to be held in Kansas City, Missouri, Sunday, March 22, 1942. Rector Earl Jewell performed the ceremony in the Saint Andrews Episcopal Church. A reception followed at the Adam home for some seventy guests. Jean, Ginny's younger sister was Maid of Honor. Bridesmaids were Miss Virginia Ruth Higley, sister of the groom, and Miss Jane Rayner Couffer, cousin of the bride. Groomsmen included Robert W. Couffer Jr., of Oak Park, Illinois, cousin of the bride, Vard Nelson and Andrew Silkyta of Kansas City. It was a short honeymoon as Ensign Higley had to return to active duty on the Wednesday after the wedding. Ginny was only nineteen and Bob was twenty-four.

Virginia's Wedding Photo

Kansas City Star Wedding Photo

Wedding Certificate

Navy Officers and Wives

BACK TO THE WAR

Repairs and reconditioning was complete on the *Ranger* on April 6, 1942. Commander of the Aircraft Atlantic Fleet, Rear Admiral Arthur Bryon Cook left the ship, and Commander Carriers Atlantic Fleet Rear Admiral E. D. Mc Whortter came aboard, retaining Cook's staff. On April 13th, The *Ranger* left the Norfolk area, arriving in Narragansett Bay the following day and mooring at the Naval Air Station pier, Ouonset Point, (The Air National Guard Station, Rhode Island) April 17th. April 22, she got underway with cargo of US Army P-40 planes and pilots. She proceeded by way of Trinidad to the Gold Coast of Africa where the P-40s flew off to Accra, Ghana. All planes landed safely on May 10th and the complete voyage was made without incident, returning by Trinidad and anchoring in Narragansett Bay on May 28th.

The British were relieved when America entered World War II in December 1941. The British hoped that the United States would soon collaborate with them in operations against the Nazis. In the 1930s Japan was at war with China, although at the time it was an undeclared war. Japan wished to gain control of the Pacific and much of Asia. The war in Europe began in 1939, when Germany invaded Poland and began to annex major portions of Europe. Once the US had declared war with Japan following the attack on Pearl Harbor, the Axis Powers declared war on the US and rushed to support Japan in the Pacific. The US and her allies, Great Britain and the Soviet Union, were faced with fighting in Europe, North Africa and the Pacific. British Prime Minister Winston Churchill under pressure from the Soviet Union's dictator Josef Stalin to open a second front, pleaded with President Franklin Roosevelt to join British forces in an invasion of the North African coast where the Germans had launched a land and sea war. Churchill specifically requested that the Ranger be sent to North Africa but it was determined that the Ranger would not be sent as she was too slow for successful maneuvering in rapid fire situations.

The British fleet included seven carriers in three task forces to cover two landing areas along the North African coast. Five American flattops joined them to make up the Western Naval Task Force. It was lead by The *Ranger*. The American forces landed at Casablanca, while two British forces landed at Oran (Center) landing area and Algiers

(Eastern) landing area. A third British Task Force covered operations in the Mediterranean, mainly to defend against any opposition from the Italians. The name of the offensive in North Africa was Operation Torch. The British fleet sailed through the Straits of Gibraltar into the Mediterranean on November 6,1942 and the Americans stayed in the Atlantic.

Bob was one of the airman, part of Squadron 41, that was to fly off the *Ranger* near the coast of North Africa. For most of the American crews this was their first combat operation and apprehension and discussion went through all the ready rooms. Bob had flown scout missions but had not experienced air combat to this point. Bob's training had begun before the U.S. entered the war.

He was older than most of the pilots that were trained in a very short time after we entered the war. The plane he flew was a Grumman TBF Avenger.

The Avenger's first combat mission was at Midway the 4th of June 1942. Six of these aircraft thundered off into the Battle of Midway and only one came back. This was not because it was a bad plane. The Avenger was to become one of the great bombers of the conflict. Developed quickly during the early stages of the war, there hadn't been much testing as they were needed yesterday.

Grumman's large single engine torpedo-bomber was patriotically and appropriately named Avenger on December 7,1941, the Day of Infamy' on which Japan attacked Pearl Harbor. Procured and constructed in great quantities the Avenger saw action with Allied air arms in virtually all theaters of operation in World War II. Of the 9,836 aircraft produced 2290 were built by Grumman (so somewhat confusingly designated TBF) while the General Motors Eastern Division produced the rest which were TBM's, the designation by which all Avengers are sometimes erroneously known. The Avenger was first flown on August 1,1941, having been designed and built in just five weeks - an incredible feet by today's standards when computer-aided designs can take a decade to perfect. The aircraft, designed for a three-man crew had an internal weapons bay to minimize drag, gun turret, and a rear defensive gun position. A hatch on the right side rear of the wing allowed access into the rear fuselage which was packed with equipment, flares, parachutes and ammunition. On the lower level, the bombardier had a folding seat from which he could either man the lower rear machine-gun, or face forward and aim the aircraft for medium-altitude level bombing. The pilot sat in a roomy and comfortable cockpit above the wing's leading edge, enjoying excellent visibility. The Avenger went on to become one of the great naval aircraft of World War II, being involved in the destruction of more than 60 Japanese war ships. It was the first US single-engined aircraft to carry the hard hitting 22inch torpedo (as well as depth charges, rockets and bombs) and was also the first to boast a power-operated gun turret. Torpedos launched by the US Navy Avengers were largely responsible for the sinking of the large Japanese battle ships Yamanto and Musashi.

The Avenger was designed to be a torpedo-bomber, but bombs were by far its primary weapons. The bomb bay could carry 12 - 100 lb. bombs or four 500 lb. bombs or two 1000 lb. bombs. The plane normally had a crew of three, pilot, bomb aimer & radio fixed gun. The pilot fired the fixed forward guns and released the torpedo. The Avenger was the largest single engine plane to fight in the Second World War with 900 horse power.

George Herbert Walker Bush was one of the youngest pilots to fly the Avenger in World War II. He was shot down near the island of Chi- Chi Jima and rescued by a submarine. Bush went on to become the 41st President of the United States. Warren (Bud) Kruck, from my home town of Boone, Iowa, also flew an Avenger and dropped a bomb down the chimney of a Japanese ship for which he was awarded a Navy Cross. After the war, Bud returned to Boone to run his father's plumbing and heating businesses, Kruck Plumbing and Heating, building it into one of Boone's most prominent companies. Our company R. H. Grabau Construction Inc. did several projects with his company and his son Steve.

Bob and Flight Crew in Front of Avenger

Avengers In Formation

Bob in Front of Avenger

By the early 1940's, the United States was involved in the war full force. The *Ranger* was used to ferry planes to North Africa as well as scout for German Subs in the Atlantic. On the way to the coast of North Africa, scout planes were sent out each day from the Ranger to search for German subs as well as any other enemy ships that might be in the area. Submarines were even seen near Bermuda. When enemy subs were spotted, planes would drop bombs if the sub was shallow, or depth charges if seen deeper.

The first mission the *Ranger* had was to ferry the P-40s to West Africa. They loaded 76 Army Warhawks to be delivered to Accra, Africa for the North Africa invasion mission. On April 28, 1942, the ship arrived at the Port of Spain, Trinidad. On April 29, the carrier left at 0630. A lecture was given on the mission to the crew. Their destination was Accra, Africa (British Gold Coast) where the Army planes were to be launched.

On May 9 1942, the carrier went through a German submarine pack with enemy subs clustered all around. American destroyers dropped depth charges left and right. Black smoke and oil slicks could be seen where the charges exploded. The planes were delivered and all seemed to go well. Bob and his crew continued to fly scout missions daily.

The *Ranger* then headed back to North America. On May 21st 1942, a sub was reported following the *Ranger*. The ship changed course and they lost the sub. A British torpedo boat in the area dropped depth charges, but it was a false alarm. The 27th of May all on ship were given General Quarters, or all hands to battle stations, because of a sub contact. Depth charges were dropped and soon an oil slick was seen on the surface and the sub was presumed to be sunk. May 28 planes dropped depth charges on presumed sub. The Ranger arrived at Quonset Point, Rhode Island, on May 28th, then sailed on to Argentia Bay, Newfoundland, and back to Quonset, Road Island.

Planes, that had been tested back in April, were then loaded onto the *Ranger* for the 57th Army Fighter Group to be used in Operation Torch in North Africa. Throughout the war carriers such as the *Ranger* were used to ferry planes across the Atlantic to be used in the European and North Africa battles.

Life on board a ship ranged between extremes, from boredom to being scared to death. The men would play cards during free time, either poker or bridge and small stakes because they did not have much money. Reading mail from home was a highlight when it came. Getting mail to the ship was often a challenge, but when it arrived, and distributed, the men were happy.

Letters were their main conduit to loved ones, family and friends. Letters also were sent home by the same slow process, but the men could not share with their families any specifics about their activities because of the ordered security of missions, ships and men. The men also experienced emotions because even when not in battle their shipmates died from accidents, planes that crashed because of rough seas, pilot error, and other equipment or technical malfunctions.

Ernest L. Crochet, who served as a Signal Man on the Bridge of the *Ranger*, the same time Bob flew off the *Ranger*, kept a journal of day to day activities and things he witnessed that happened on board or sightings near the carrier. He served on the *Ranger* for 52 months and 21 days for the most part outside the continental limits of the United States until August 1946

Many of Crochet's observations give a glimpse into where the ship was and what was happening at the time.

> On July 1st 1942 the Ranger left Quonset Pt. heading south. Ten days later on July 11th there were a number of sub contacts and depth charges were dropped on subs shadowing the ship.

> On July, 19th the P-40s were launched from about 100 miles out to Africa-Middle East Wing headquarters in Accra, British Gold Coast, making a total of 4 flights, (72 planes). On July 22, 1942 escort destroyers made three sub contacts. Depth charges were dropped. A scout SB2U plane attempting to land crashed, killing the pilot, but the gunner was recovered. A service was held for Lt.(jg) John Wagner the deceased pilot.

By August the carrier had returned to Norfolk, Virginia. Bob and Ginny were able to spend some time together even though Bob was on full duty. It is not clear when Ginny told Bob they were going to be parents but he was overjoyed and by that time Ginny was almost three months pregnant. The obstetrics practice did not have ultra-sound back then, so, the excited parents were left to guess, that the baby would be due in February of "43. Bob, of course had no idea where he would be when the child arrived, but he had a strong faith as indicated in his letters to Ginny, and knew things would work out.

Back on ship, once his land service in North Africa was complete, Bob and his crew mates experienced a few incidents which put their lives at risk. Signalman Crochet put the following in his journal:

> Aug. 23, 1942 Carrier left Norfolk. A Wildcat (F4F) rolled in port stacks, Pilot OK. Plane was shoved overboard. Crewman had a few cuts with propeller.

> Aug. 31 Scout bomber (SBD) crashed in barrier and turned over. Pilot OK. Fighter crashed in barriers over on nose. Pilot OK.

> Oct. 3, "42, Rough seas. F4F barrier crashed and had two busted landing gear.

> On Oct. 6th they reached Bermuda. The USS Charger lost one F4F while catapulting at anchor. No wind, Pilot OK. Two F4F busted wheels while landing, and one more busted landing gear.

> On Oct. 20th there was an accident on the USS Swannee, two men were injured and two drowned. Warships from US were coming in every day. Something BIG is coming up!

PARTICIPATION IN OPERATION TORCH _____ North Africa

On Oct. 24th, The Task Force of which the Ranger was a part, left Bermuda for operations. In Signalman Crochet's journal it was stated that an F4F crashed in the barrier and flipped on it's back. The pilot was OK. The Captain spoke of the mission-supporting the invasion of North Africa. The Task Force sailed toward North Africa, which at the time was the greatest movement of ships and men by sea in history. The convoy stretched for 25 miles. The strike into North Africa in November 1942 was intended to draw Axis forces away from the Eastern Front, thus relieving pressure on the hard-pressed Soviet Union. The operation was a compromise between U.S. and British planners as the latter felt that the American-advocated landing in northern Europe was premature and would lead to disaster at this stage of the war.

The operation was planned as a pincer movement, or double envelopment, in which forces simultaneously attack both flanks of an enemy formation with U.S. landings on Morocco's Atlantic coast (Western Task Force-Safi, Fedala, Mehdla-Port Lyautey) and Anglo-American landings on Algeria's Mediterranean coast(Center and Eastern task forces- Oran, Algiers) There was also a battalion-sized airborne landing near Oran with the mission to seize two airfields. The primary objective of the Allied landings was to secure bridgeheads for opening a second front to the rear of the German and Italian forces battling the British in Libya and Egypt. However, resistance by the normally neutral or potentially pro-German Vichy French forces needed to be overcome first. After a transatlantic crossing, the Western Task Force effected its landing on November 8th.

A preliminary naval bombardment had been deemed unnecessary in the vain hope that French forces would not resist. In fact, the initially stiff French defense caused losses among the landing forces. Lieutenant (jg) Higley was part of Scouting Squadron Forty-one. This was his first flight into battle of both enemy planes and ground based antiaircraft guns. His preparation for the flight was excellent. Bob's log book revealed he had flown over 700 hours in different planes from his early training until his mission at Casablanca. He had dropped bombs on enemy subs as well as flown near hostel ships on scouting missions. This mission was different, and Bob prayed he was ready for what ever came his way. He also felt the responsibility of his crew, which in this case was a sailor named Colon. (name in Bob's Log Book) Between the 8th and 11th of November,1942, they flew 12.5 hours of combat. In Bob's first experience flying in combat he did himself and the Navy proud. They accomplished their mission and the plane and crew came back to the ship alive. However by 10 November, all landing objectives had been accomplished and U.S. units were poised to assault Casablanca, whose harbor approaches were the scene of a brief but fierce, naval engagement. The French surrendered the city before an all-out attack was launched. Following the successful completion of OPERATION TORCH, a letter of commendation was sent to Lt.(jg) Robert H. Higley.

RESTRICTED

VS41/P15   December 11, 1942.

From: Commander, Scouting Squadron FORTY ONE.
To :   Lieutenant (jg) Robert H. HIGLEY, U. S. Naval Reserve.

Subject: Commendation for excellent performance of duty
           in action against the enemy.

References: (a) Commander Task Group 34.2 despatch 081758 of
                November, 1942.
            (b) Commander Task Group 34.2 despatch of November
                10, 1942.
            (c) Commander Task Group 34.2 despatch of November
                11, 1942.

     1.   References (a), (b) and (c) are quoted herewith:

           Reference (a):
             From: Commander Task Group 34.2.
             To : RANGER and RANGER Air Group.

           The outstanding performance of the RANGER and
           RANGER Air Group on Sunday, November 8, 1942
           surpasses any known achievement by a carrier
           and its Air Group. The cheerful and willing
           manner in which pilots took off on a total of
           two hundred and three flights to engage the
           enemy constitutes a bright page in the history
           of the RANGER. The efficient handling of
           planes and ship by the officers and crew of
           the RANGER made this remarkable performance
           possible. Several men have made the supreme
           sacrifice in fighting our country's cause but
           our aircraft have made a major contribution
           to the successful landings by Army troops at
           Fedala and Port Lyautey. I take pleasure in
           saying quote well done unquote

                              McWHORTER

           Reference (b):
             From: Commander Task Group 34.2.
             To : RANGER and RANGER Air Group.

           Your continued efficiency and effective opera-
           tions are an inspiration to all. Again well
           done RANGER and RANGER Air Group.

53

Although not over, by the summer of 1942, the battle in North Africa was moving to the East and Allied ground troops and tanks were pursuing the Germans and their General Johannes Eugene Rommel, "The Desert Fox," who commanded the very battle ready tanks, Panzerarmee. High ranking allied officers in North Africa included American General George Patton, and Dwight D. Eisenhower, as well as British General Montgomery. Eisenhower was put in charge of "Operation Torch," but it took a while for him to gain the respect of General Montgomery. Montgomery said of his new boss, General Eisenhower, "Good chap— no soldier! He knows nothing whatever about how to make war or fight battles; he should be kept right away from all that business if he wants to win this war." Because of all the different leaders and allies fighting together, politics had to be handled, as well as fighting. I think President Roosevelt felt Ike was a steady leader to control the ego's of the other generals. He was "baptized by fire" so the name "Operation Torch" came to have more than one meaning.

Besides providing air support from Navy Pilots the Ranger continued to ferry Army Planes to Africa. The ship and her consort of planes headed back to the states on November 14th, 1942.

Ernest L. Crochet's, the Ranger's signalman, wrote in his journal, an account of that return trip:

> November 9,1942 Following is a brief summary of yesterdays air operations X
>
> Airfields at Lyautey and Casa Blanca immobilized X Air coverage furnished landing parties X Our loses 13 planes and pilots missing X 9 more crashed near ships but all personnel recovered X Situation safe excellent transport now unloading at dock X Bernadou (DD) and Cole (DD) rushed dock without causalities X Landings at Lyautey and Fedala encountered some resistance but seemed to be well in hand at last observation X Naval forces at Casa Blanca determined to resist.
>
> Nov.10, 1942 From Ranger to All Ships Present: 9

Scouts just returned from blasting Jean Bartwith 7 1000-lb bomb hits by special requests after Bart opened up on Mighty with turret salvos X VF9 ran interference.

Nov.11,1942. From Swannee (CVE) to Ranger: Intelligence summery 1200 eleventh X VGS 27 sank submarine believed to be German of 740 tons at 0710 11th.

X Sub was crash diving when struck by 8 depth charges X Position approximately 15 miles west of Casa Blanca.

Nov. 14, 1942 From Ranger to All Ships: We are homeward bound X Our screen is very thin X

The upmost alertness by all hands will be required to get us through safely X You have done a grand job don't relax now.

Nov. 17, 1942 Ranger refueling. Strange ship sighted and investigated. Proved to be friendly. 1942 Arrived in Bermuda and anchored. Great Sound 10:15.

Nov. 22, 1942 Left Bermuda at 13:30 for States

Nov. 25, 1942 Arrive Norfolk and moor Pier 7 at 13:40

Dec. 3,1942 In and out of operations. Torpedo plane (TBF) rolled in catwalk, Pilot OK. A second YBF rolled over on stacks.

Dec. 25,1942 First Christmas home.

The United States probably had never looked so good to Bob. He had been married to Ginny now for nine months, but they had not been able to spend much time together. Ginny was expecting their first child. Christmas was one day off. It was great to spend it with Ginny at their apartment on base in Norfolk, Virginia.

By that Christmas, war was raging all over the world and there was no escaping it's effect at home as well as abroad. Many commodities were scarce because of the war, so rationing was strictly enforced. War Ration books were purchased to allow those at home to purchase certain items that were in short supply. Americans had to save their rations in order to buy what they needed. These included rubber tires, nylon stockings, fuel, and even certain types of food and commodities. Metals, including, steel, copper and brass were used for ammunition as well as manufacturing of ships, planes, and war trucks, tanks and other transport vehicles. War bonds were sold to finance the war effort. While in Norfolk, Bob continued training from Norfolk, for what ever would be his next assignment. The US Troops were now fighting in Europe and the South Pacific.

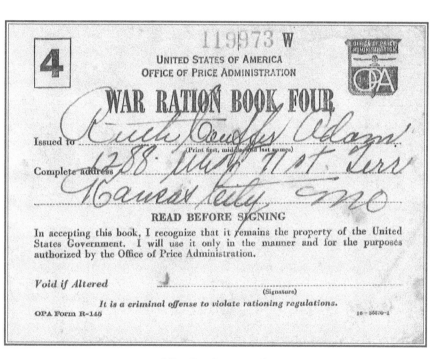

War Ration Book

NEW PARENTS: SHARON JEAN HIGLEY IS BORN

During Bob's training period, Ginny gave birth to a little girl on February 9th, 1943 in Norfolk, Virginia. Her proud parents named her Sharon Jean Higley (Sherry) and as we all know a new baby also really changes peoples' lives. The name Sharon was one of the most popular names chosen for baby girls born in World War II. Being born in war time can be very scary for both parents. One important outcome of having a child during wartime, it gives the mother a needed and concrete focus for her life. She has less time to worry about the 'what if's.

A new baby also provided a necessary distraction for its excited father. Ginny was a wonderful mother and Sherry was her "little princess". Ginny's mother, Ruth, had raised her daughters well, she had taught them to trust in God, respect others, and express gratitude.

Bob & Ginny with baby Sherry

While in Norfolk, Bob had some time off and even was able to play some golf. Although still training, he had time to clear his head of the fighting behind him as well as in front of him. Bob and Ginny weren't able to go very far, but they did take some short trips to get some relaxation. During those precious days Ginny began to keep even the smallest reminders of their time together. In her scrap books were match book covers and napkins and other momentos from many of the short times they were able to spend together.

Bob's Silver Star was presented on March 24, 1943, at a ceremony in an aircraft hanger at the Navy Base for his flying in Operation Torch in North Africa. Lieutenant Robert Higley along with several other soldiers received awards for exceptional bravery and service.

The Silver Star's history changed at the beginning of World War II. The newly-established (1932) Medal was still exclusively a U. S. Army (War Department) award. For this reason, most of the earliest WWII awards to members of all branches of service were presented by the Army. For their heroism on December 7, 1941, at Pearl Harbor, 49 members of the Army and Army Air Force received the first Silver Stars of the war. When General Douglas MacArthur presented Silver Stars to Marine private Alexander Katchuck and Private First Class Charles Greer for their actions in the Philippine Islands on December 29, 1941, the two men became the First Marines of World War II to receive the Silver Star.

Army awards of the Silver Star were awarded to additional Marines, and U. S. Naval personnel early in 1942, the majority for gallantry in the Philippine Islands prior to the fall of Corregidor. The fact that the Silver Star was solely an Army award explains why, though members of the Navy earned USN/USMC Pearl Harbor heroes received the Navy marine Corps Medal. On August 7, 1942, nearly a year after World War II began, by Act of Congress in Public Law 702, (77th Congress) award of the Silver Star was expanded to the Navy. Ultimately, three members of the Navy and one Marine were presented the Navy Silver Star for their actions at Pearl Harbor.

Lt. Higley's Citation read as follows: The President of the United States take pleasure in presenting the Silver Star Medal to Lieutenant Robert Higley, United States Navy, for service as set forth in the following Citation:

For conspicuous gallantry and intrepidity as pilot of an airplane in Scouting Squadron Forty-ONE attached to the *U.S.S. RANGER*, during the occupation of French Morocco, November 8-11, 1942. Participating in numerous flight missions against the enemy, Lieutenant (jg) Higley pressed home his attacks with bold determination and utter disregard for his own personal safety. In the face of tremendous anti- aircraft fire, he took part in an effective air raid on heavy gun emplacements and later, as a member of a flight of nine planes, dive-bombed a hostel battle-ship. His superb flying skill and conscientious devotion to duty were in keeping with the highest tradition of the United States Naval Service.

Signed by Frank Knox
For the President,
Secretary of the Navy

Bob Higley Awarded Silver Star

Avenger in Flight

Bob's Log Book

KEY TO LOG
ABBREVIATIONS

A   - Training (Regular
      Students
A-1 - Basic Instruction
      (Midshipmen)
A-2 - Elimination Train-
      ing (Regulars)
A-3 - Familiarization
      (Non-aviation)
B   - Training (Reserve
      Students)
B-2 - Elimination Train-
      ing (Reserves)
C   - Training (Qualified
      Pilots)
D   - Reserve Flying
E   - Familiarization
F   - Gunnery
G   - Bombing
H   - Torpedo
I   - Observation
J   - Scouting
K   - Tactical
L   - Navigation
M   - Transportation
N   - Ferrying
O   - Utility
P   - Photographic
Q   - Aerological
R   - Test
S   - Experimental
T   - Administrative
U   - Extended
V   - Instrument
W   - Emergency
X   - Communication
Y   - Night Flying
Z   - Special

Log Book Codes

65

Ginny carefully clipped all the articles about Bob's service award and glued them in her scrap book. Next to these articles were other memorabilia from their time together, including one special Easter card with the message, Happy Easter Hubby, I know there is a Santa Claus, and an Easter Bunny too, I got them both rolled into one the day I married you! Happy Easter darling-signed, "with love, Ginny."

Ginny not only had her husband to worry about but also her father had reenlisted in the Marines. James Adam had been one of the first men from Oak Park, Illinois to enlist for service in World War I, just five days after war was declared, in April 1917. He served two and a half years in the Marines before being discharged. He and his wife, Ruth had moved to Kansas City, Missouri in the early 1930's.

He now reenlisted in the Marines and was promoted to the rank of Captain. He was stationed in Quantico, Virginia, where Marine Officers were trained. He was later stationed at Grove City, Pennsylvania.

When Bob was in port, he, Ginny, and their new daughter Sherry stayed in Base Housing for a cost of $30 per month. They spent as much time together as a family as possible. That summer they were able to take a short vacation to New York City by having Ginny's mother, Ruth, come and take care of little Sherry, now a little over four months old. The trip allowed them to see Ginny's relatives who lived near the city as well as to have some time alone. They went first class and stayed at the Waldorf Astoria on Park Avenue and Fiftieth Street in New York City. Ginny saved the hotel receipt, which showed they paid $7.00 per night. They were there from June 10th until June 14,1943. This may have been when my wife was conceived, based on the time line.

While in the city they went to LEON & EDDIES, where you could order a complete Table D'Hote Dinner served daily from 5-10 P.M. beginning at $1.50. The advertisement for the restaurant found in Ginny's scrapbook, also had a place for autographs and a soldier at the bottom encouraging customers to BUY WAR BONDS! Ginny also saved a napkin from The Waldorf Astoria with drawings of the decorations in the TONY SARG OASIS ROOM. I also found napkins as well from Cafe Trouville and The Monkey Bar located in The Hotel Elysee on 60 E.54th Street. Ginny collected match book covers and pasted them into her scrapbook from The Madison and Arnando's.

They attended church at NYC's St. Bartholomew's Church, as a bulletin glued in her scrap book attests. Ginny saved programs from The Playbill and THE MUSIC BOX, where they saw and heard Michael Todds's STAR and GARTER performances that they enjoyed while in New York. They sat in really good seats near the orchestra that cost $2.00 each. They had a great time in New York and were at times even able to forget that the war was going on. Only too quickly they had to return to reality.

Bob was soon back to training flights, in Norfolk, while he waited for his next assignment. He and Ginny were able to spend time together in the evenings and once even took a short road trip to North Carolina. They stayed at Mayview Manor in Blowing Rock, North Carolina. Bob golfed with a Navy captain and they had Ginny keep score. Ginny even saved the score card which showed Bob scoring a 42 on the front nine and 45 on the back nine. He beat the captain by four strokes. They also hiked and were able to relax at least for a short time.

Ginny and Bob

Waldorf Hotel New York City

MEMO.		DATE	EXPLANATION		AMT. CHARGED		AMT. CREDITED	BAL. D
	1	JUN10-43	ROOM		☆	7.00		☆
	2	JUN11-43	VALET		☆	2.25		☆
	3	JUN11-43	PHONE-LD		☆	0.41		☆
	4	JUN11-43	ROOM		☆	7.00		☆
	5	JUN11-43	PHONE		☆	0.11		☆ 1
	6	JUN12-43	ROOM		☆	7.00		☆ 2
	7	JUN13-43	ROOM		☆	7.00		☆
	8							
	9							
	10							
	11							
	12							
	13							
	14							
	15							
	16							
	17							
	18							
	19							
	20							
	21							
	22							

1766 HIGLEY LT R H & MRS 7-00 SPL
U S NAVY NORFOLK VA
7315 W KENMORE DR
6-10J   10-08PMPC

The WALDORF·ASTORIA
NEW YORK

Waldorf Bill

Bob and Ginny in New York

In Norfolk, Bob continued training and was assigned to a new aircraft carrier called the *Bunker Hill*. She was named after The Battle of Bunker Hill in the American Revolutionary War. The carrier was one of 24 Essex-class aircraft carriers built during World War II for the United States Navy. She was built by Bethlehem Steel Company's Fore River Shipyard, Quincy, Massachusetts and launched December 7, 1942. Her displacement was 27,100 tons standard and 36,380 ton with full load. Her length was 820 feet at the waterline, and 147'-6' overall. Her beam was 93' at waterline with a flight deck of 147'-5". She was powered by 8x Babcock & Wilcox Boilers at 150,000 horsepower. Propulsion consisted of 4x shafts: 4x geared steam turbines. Her speed was 33 knots, or about 38 mph. The carrier's range was 14,100 mmi, or about 16,200 miles at 20 knots. Her complement was 2600. Armament included: 4x twin 5 inch 38 caliber guns, 4x single 5 inch 38 caliber guns, 8x quadruple 40 mm 56 caliberguns and 46x single 20mm 78 caliber guns. The *Bunker Hill* was laid down September 15, 1941, and launched less than a year later, on December 7, 1942. She was Commissioned May 25, 1943.

The motto of the ship became: *NEVER SURRENDER, NEVER SINK,* and her nickname became "HOLIDAY EXPRESS". Captain J.J. Ballentine was the Officer in command. Bob Higley was part of the air group that went aboard at the end of June at Norfolk, Virginia. On the 15th of July, they sailed south to Trinidad on her shakedown cruise. Three weeks later the ship returned to Norfolk, and on September 4, 1943 it sailed south to the Panama Canal on the way to San Diego, Pearl Harbor, and the Pacific Theater of Operations. One of the reasons the Ranger was not sent back into the Pacific is that she was older and too slow.

The Bunker Hill

The Bunker Hill with blimp

The *Bunker Hill* had worked up with VF-17, a new fighter squadron flying F4U Corsairs. The Corsairs, a new airplane, had some difficulties in its development, and the navy gave consideration to replacing VF-17's Corsairs with Grumman F6 Hellcats. The squadron successfully argued for retention of it's Corsairs, as they felt they were better combat aircraft. Hence Bunker Hill had departed for the combat theater with it's VF-17 Corsairs aboard. While on route from San Diego to Pearl Harbor, the pilots found out that the Navy had decided not to use Corsairs aboard carriers to avoid carrying parts and supplies for both (the Corsair and the Hellcat) and because of the challenges the US Navy was having in getting Corsairs approved for carrier use at that time. It wasn't until 1944 that a landing technique was developed to land the Corsairs safely on the deck of carriers. Bob Higley flew a few times with a F4FU for training according to his log but for the most part he flew TBF-1 planes.

Before they sailed for Rabaul Harbor, New Britain, Bob spent a little time on the Hawaiian Island of Oahu where Pearl Harbor is located. He sent Ginny a gift and had to write a letter stating that it was a gift garment and worth less that fifty $50. This note found in Ginny's scrapbook was dated October 17, 1943 and signed R.H. Higley Lieutenant USN. He also sent a typed letter to Ginny on the back of a colored map of the Hawaii Islands In hope they might return someday after the war. He even wrote about the Hawaiian language and how some words were pronounced. It was as if he was trying to teach the pronunciation of some of the common words, and he took what he learned during his short stay very serious. He thought the best word he had learned was "aloha", writing: "you will find it at the end of this letter. It means much more than just goodbye, It's "hello." "love to you", "good morning", "how ya doing?" or any kind of pleasant greeting."

In his letter, Bob also wrote "you ought to see the miles of green sugar cane on the islands. That's where a lot of sugar for Uncle Sam's fighting forces comes from. Well (hot) one for the book: before the cane is cut they set the fields on fire! This burns the heavy leaves and makes the crop easier to harvest, but doesn't hurt the cane." The letter was typed on the back side of the small map of the Hawaiian Islands showing the names of all the separate islands. Bob apologized for his typing but said he could get more on a page by typing. He closed with, "Aloha nui" which means "I love you big." in Hawaiian.

BUNKER HILL SAILS TOWARDS THE SOUTHWEST PACIFIC

Rabaul is located just a little above New Guinea and is sheltered by mountains on one side and a narrow access on the other. The Japanese had made this a "Pearl Harbor" or a safe harbor for their ships and they had fortified it very well with antiaircraft guns to make it difficult to attack. The following was a written account in the *Bunker Hill* Year Book that Ginny kept in a trunk in her attic for many years.

RABAUL

Dawn—November 11,1943; the longest day of our life. It all comes back in the form of mental flashes drawn from a brain file of a vivid pictures that now yellow in an ash heap of memory. We won't forget it. In America, Armistice bands played for holiday parades, and strings of confetti fell like well-wishes from heaven. A cold wind swept the streets of Chicago, and brilliant, warmish sun lay to the heart of Texas; The lemon light of East Forty-Second Street was hardly enough to ward off chill winds that swept up from the man-made canyons of Lower Manhattan; and in Georgia the last locks of cotton were being packed into burlap bags by husky Negros who sang about Glory and Hallelujah as they worked.

That was back home. You have forgotten it by now. This is out here: a small force of carriers and destroyers streaked northward and westward through warm, tropical waters, their grayish stacks shimmering in the diffused light of a bright moon, that sifted its way through a white skin of clouds. It was an hour before sunrise and you could hardly discern where the moonlight ended and the bluish twilight began. Sailors were going to their battle stations; pilots were climbing into their planes; the bell muzzles of dozens of ready guns pointed solemnly into the winey air of a tropical dawn. Everywhere there was an electrical current flowing and ebbing through the blood of a new crew that waited to fight a new ship. Through the minds of these 3000 men there ran a human movie tone of mystery and excitement; they were waiting to meet an enemy they had never seen, an enemy they had sailed thousands of miles to face. Today was the first day; it was the beginning of time; it was the epitome of fanfare and trumpets, of startling noises and sicking smells, of man's roaring mechanics made to fend off his enemies, of a small kid's willingness to pray — even after he becomes a grown man.

That was out here, and we remember it even though its sharper edges have dulled, exposed to the acids of time. That was the beginning from the very moment the first pilot rattled the flaps on his dive bomber's wings to make certain they were ready. When zero hour came, you seemed to know it without having to be told. Everything turned quiet for a full minute, just as in a small school room back in Ohio, all the kids were quiet and respectful for one minute at eleven o'clock on America's Armistice Day back home. When everything was quiet there came a voice over the air, a voice that was heavy with feelings for our fates. It said a prayer-aloud, and it asked God to bless us and our ship.

And then time began moving clockwise. A simultaneous whir of propellers signaled the beginning of a mission, our first. The roar of dozens of engines, their exhaust wakes leaving the semi-light of early morning spotted with green and blue fireflies. One by one the fighters were rolling off the flight deck, followed by dive bombers and then torpedo planes. Soon the air was alive with buzzing, droning noises that circled our formation, came together, and turned the nose of a perfect V toward the target for the day, our first target. They would be over Rabaul Harbor in little more than an hour. Rabaul with its suggestive qualities: Japanese ships at anchor, hundreds of antiaircraft guns that lined the hook shaped estuary, and dozens of airfields that, by dawn, would be sending hundreds of the Emperor's finest bird men soaring into the Emperor's own unchaste sky.

There will never be anything quite like it. That day- the longest day of our life-stands out not only as the ship's first action, a baptism by fire to take its place among the great battles of the war, but for its defensive brilliance. On this ship Rabaul will be remembered most for the manner in which our squadrons and ships repelled wave after wave of enemy planes in one of the most vicious and prolonged attacks then on record. It all came about as an unscheduled sideshow not many days prior to the invasion of the Gilbert Islands. Leaving our Pacific headquarters we were told of the role we were to play in that invasion. You could hardly detect signs of approaching battle among the crew; it was still something vague and far away. Sun-bathing and flight deck sports- they were more like reality. Battle was tomorrow, something that would likely never come.

Yet in less than two weeks the Baby of Quincy, (*Bunker Hill*) was cutting her teeth in glorious battle against the enemy, having her flight deck drenched with salt water geysered up by near misses and seeing her own children countered with death and destruction from the onslaughts of the Nippon tide.

The day before November 11, 1942 was strangely monotonous. Routine duties filled our daily schedule. Having never been through battle the vision of our foe were somewhat unreal, almost nonexistent. At nightfall the atmosphere tensed up however, men about the deck saw loading preparations under way: huge bombs, deadly torpedoes, tons of aircraft ammunition— nothing could be left undone. The Captain spoke… that brought us closer still to what waited us tomorrow:

"We're steaming up the slot tonight," he said, "—the slot so famous for its battles for Guadalcanal (the shores of the Solomons had been sighted at noon that day)—for the chance we've all been waiting for. (Training days, towed sleeves… lifeless target sleds, friendly dogfights.) We've been asked to help out on a little job at Rabaul, and we'll contact the enemy in the morning. (Photographic planes have given weird descriptions this New Britain base, it's landlocked harbor, it's numerous associated air fields. Rabaul—it was a fearful name, after all.)

I have every confidence that each and every one of you will do his duty…" It was just after sunset and the twilight suddenly acquired mysterious expectations for tomorrow, a day that seemed vaguely unreal. Pilots had been briefed; dinner was served. Though it was hot and sultry below decks, the battle dinner was nothing short of a harvest feast. Viewing the kingly setting, Ensign Charley Husted was heard to remark: "I hope this isn't the Last Supper…" For Charley it was: his plane went down in flames and he was forced to parachute down over the target into a storm of strafing Jap planes.

Tomorrow did come. For breakfast all hands had beefsteak, and at 0645 sixty-nine pilots and their crewman took off in twenty-seven Hellcats, twenty-three Hell divers and nineteen Avengers. Forced to the sidelines because his Avenger engine was skipping, Lieutenant Bob Higley saw his teammates soar off the carrier to blend with the dawn. Thinking that he alone would have to wait and "sweat them out." Before the flight had rendezvoused, his plane was in commission, and he took off, a solitary figure in the cockpit of his plane, the typical American fighting man that he was-and that's the last memory we have of that gallant airman. He was never seen in the vicinity of the target, and it was feared that he fell victim to jackal Zekes on the lurk for stragglers.

We will never know exactly what happened to Bob and his crew that day. He was not seen in the battle but most pilots aren't looking for their fellow pilots. They had enough to do just keep themselves out of harms way. He could have had engine trouble again as his plane had trouble before he took off. He may have made it to his target and then was shot down. Pilots are taught what to do if in trouble in the air, but just like Nile Kinnick, it doesn't always save them. Bob was a decorated naval officer and had been tested before in combat. I would guess most of the pilots had not been in actual combat before being assigned to the *Bunker Hill*. When the ship personal realized he had not come back, they could only hope he had ditched safely and made it to shore or had been picked up by another allied ship. His last letter home was on its way back to Ginny, but as it takes a while for mail to travel back from that distance, it did not reach her before she found out he was missing in action.

Virginia (Ginny) later in life, would often say that Bob never should have been sent into battle late, and not with the rest of his squadron. We don't know if that was his decision or an order. My guess is that he did not want to let his squadron down and hoped he could catch up with them.

Virginia raised her family very cautiously, and some of that came from loosing Bob early in their marriage. She would often say, "I was born on Friday the thirteenth and I have been unlucky ever since." She had many examples of "bad" things that could happen if her children didn't follow her safety advice. When her family grew older she was often the target of "funny" stories of these cautious moments. My wife used to say she wasn't allowed to cross the street by herself until she was at least eighteen years old. I would tell Nancy that even though Virginia's life was sad from the loss of Bob he gave Ginny two beautiful daughters and she was later blessed with three more children that made her life complete.

This letter was in too bad of shape to scan so I retyped it. It was dated November 4,1943 or one week before Rabaul when Bob went missing. Bob wrote this letter to his parents.

80

Nov. 4,1943

Dear Folks,

I guess you have been wondering if I fell off the end of the world or something. I would have written sooner but there is so little to write about and the spirit seldom moves me. The last letter I had from you all was marked October 8 so you can readily see I am not too up to date on any news you may have written. We all take turns flying patrols and then sit around the rest of the day wondering what to do. Of course now and then we do have some sort of intelligence lecture. Every evening there is the usual bridge game in the ward room. My luck has been pretty poor lately and I'm down a little. We usually play for a tenth and get in about 6 rubbers, some of the boys play every day. I have been laying off for a couple of days after they nicked me.

I have run across a number of boys on here from K.C. Jack Hasburg for one, I believe he lives out our way somewhere. George Weber, whose mother lives over on Linwood. At present I'm living with Jim Wilson who lives in Washington but came from Bethany. he used to be with the Department of Justice until he came in the Navy a little over a year ago, a very nice fellow and we get along fine. That guy Kridel finally got unbearable so I got rid of him. Jim Wilson is a good friend of Sam Trustee who I believe I've heard Dad mention. There are lots of others I run across them every day. We have quite a bull session about the home town. As a whole the ship has a very good bunch of people. Naturally we could all think of better places to be but make the best of the situation at hand. You'll most likely be reading about us one of these days.

I found out the other day that my time in the National Guard counts for a fogey. That is 5% for each three years of service. So in time I'll get back pay to June 1942 and draw the extra 5%. I also completed 3 years Navy service. on Oct. 15 so will get another 5%. That ain't hay and will amount to a goodly sum. The funny part is I used to work like the devil for a couple of dollars a week over at the armory and now it pays me about $15 a month just for having been in.

The magazines on here are getting quite stale. However, if you get snooping around in some of the rooms you sometimes run into one you haven't read. I happened to find an Aug. Cosmo that was new to me so have been reading it quite thoroughly. Speaking of magazines, you probably wouldn't guess it but we use the National Geographic for lots of intelligence information. You can hardly put your finger on any place in the world that can't be looked up in the Geographic. They may be a little old but the land does not change and neither do the people.

I guess I'm just about as far away from you as I can possibly get. I was just trying to figure out what time it is there and I think it is about 7 o'clock last night. Rather queer to stop and think this war is going on clear around the clock and that we are fighting to uphold American ideals in every corner of the globe. I can assure you I will be glad when it is all over.

There is still no place like the USA and if anyone says there is their nuts.

I could probably sit here and wrack my brain for a while more but believe I shall close for the present. Give my best to all and remember I'm thinking about you.

Signed, Love, Bob

Monday, Nov. 8, 1943

My darling Ginny,

Well darling, I really hit the jack-pot as far as mail is concerned. It was about time however, as we had received none for about three weeks. Among the many were thirteen of your wonderful letters, one from my young daughter, one each from Mom, Dad and Sis and one from Jim. It took me quite a while to read all of them and you may rest assured that each was thoroughly read.

Naturally the ones from you were the high spots. I am so glad you are making out so well and hope that things continue to go on. From your letters, I can almost see our young daughter progressing. She is quite the young lady to be crawling around and talking. First thing you know she will be up and walking around and getting into everything. Gosh I sure would like to see her. The pictures you spoke of weren't in the mail that came aboard but may come in today. I sure hope so as I would like to see them.

It sounds like you are having some real winter weather and would I like to be there. I imagine after being out here I probably wouldn't be able to stand much cold weather. I would like to have seen Sherry's expression when she saw a snow storm. I'll bet she was really cute. That little snow-suit sounds like just the thing, but I'll bet she doesn't like all that wool around her.

From your descriptions, you are probably having quite a time with your clothes. Guess it is getting to be quite a problem. Our estimate of the time of arrival was evidently off as I didn't think it would be until next March or April. I don't think however that it will be any birthday present for Sherry. Do you have arrangements made for hospital etc. I guess that is quite a problem. I am really thrilled darling and hope that you are too. I only wish that I could be with you as I was last time. If I'm not though you will know that I'm pulling for you and am beside you in spirit anyway. Just as you are beside me always. They may separate us physically, but spiritually they will never part us. Our love extends across the miles until we are

Bob's Last letter to Ginny

83

like one person.

There has been a short interlude since I started this letter. I went visiting and saw Chas. Iarrobino. He is on the job that is with us. Saw quite a number of fellows but don't believe you know any of them. Your dope about Mal was quite right, but he is back again and I can see his job from here. They were in Dago when we left but I missed him. We traded all the latest dope and tried to find out where everyone was.

When I got back there were two more of your letters waiting for me and one had the pictures of Sherry. They are really cute and I have been showing them to everyone. Also had a couple of packages. One from the gang at the mill where I used to work and the other a box of candy from your Mother. I will have to acknowledge for all that later on as this letter will just make the mail if possible. I thought the picture of you was very good and was sure glad to getit. The young lady looks just as chubby as ever to me but it is hard to tell from pictures.

Sorry you are having trouble with the car. It seems like we always get a lemon someway or other. I guess the only thing to do is just keep repairing the darn thing as long as it runs. I'm sure we won't lose anything on our investment.

I expect I had better close this as I do want it to leave the ship. I miss you my darling and love you so much. It would be wonderful if we could be together but that will have to wait for awhile. I'll dream of you darling and be thinking of you as always.

Forever your,

Bob

Last Letter continued

84

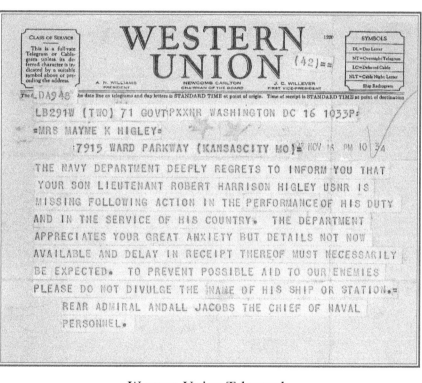

LB291W (TWO) 71 GOVT PXXNR WASHINGTON DC 16 1033P:

=MRS MAYME K HIGLEY=

7915 WARD PARKWAY (KANSASCITY MO) NOV 16 PM 10 34

THE NAVY DEPARTMENT DEEPLY REGRETS TO INFORM YOU THAT
YOUR SON LIEUTENANT ROBERT HARRISON HIGLEY USNR IS
MISSING FOLLOWING ACTION IN THE PERFORMANCE OF HIS DUTY
AND IN THE SERVICE OF HIS COUNTRY. THE DEPARTMENT
APPRECIATES YOUR GREAT ANXIETY BUT DETAILS NOT NOW
AVAILABLE AND DELAY IN RECEIPT THEREOF MUST NECESSARILY
BE EXPECTED. TO PREVENT POSSIBLE AID TO OUR ENEMIES
PLEASE DO NOT DIVULGE THE NAME OF HIS SHIP OR STATION.=
REAR ADMIRAL ANDALL JACOBS THE CHIEF OF NAVAL
PERSONNEL.

Western Union Telegraph

U. S. S. BUNKER HILL

c/o Fleet Post Office,
San Francisco, Calif.,
November 11, 1943.

My dear Mrs. Higley,

I wish to express to you and the members of the family my deepest sympathy in regard to your husband who is missing in action. He failed to return from a flight today while performing his duty in attacking the enemy. No one actually saw Bob go in, so there is the hope, which we fervently cherish, that he may still be alive and that a report of his rescue may yet reach us. In these uncertain days I want you to know that we share your heavy anxiety.

Your husband's keen interest in the Navy, and the excellent manner in which he carried out his duties had won for him the high regard of his associates. His loyalty, courage, and fine character gained for him the affection of all those who had the good fortune to know him personally. Bob is the type of young man that the Navy can ill afford to lose, and he will be greatly missed by all of us.

I knew your husband well personally. We were old shipmates in the Ranger. I have always considered him an excellent pilot and a young man of sterling character and the kind of an officer we need in Naval Aviation. For this reason, please believe me Mrs. Higley, it is extremely difficult for me to send you this sad message.

While there can be no consolation for the loss of a loved one, it is hoped that you may derive some comfort, as time goes by, in knowing that Bob was lost in the service of his country and that his loss contributes to the victory over our enemies which we are determined to win as soon as possible.

If there is anything that I may do to be of assistance to you in your worry and sorrow, please do not hesitate to let me know.

In closing, I desire to extend to you, on behalf of all the officers and the men of this ship, our deepest sympathy, and again express the fervent hope that Bob has been rescued.

Very sincerely yours,

J. J. BALLENTINE,
Captain, U.S. Navy,
Commanding.

Mrs. Robert Harrison Higley
c/o Capt. S. M. Adam, U.S.M.C.R.
Naval Training School,
Grove City, Pennsylvania.

Letter from Bunker Hill Captain Ballentine

U. S. S. BUNKER HILL CV17

Fleet Post Office
San Francisco, Calif.
26 November 1943.

Mrs. Virginia Higley
7315 W. Kenmore Drive
Norfolk, Va.

Dear Mrs. Higley:

Just a line or two to extend our sincere
sympathy to you in the loss, temporary we sincerely hope,
of your husband and our shipmate, Bob.

Speaking for the ship's officers as well as
myself, I can assure you that his absence is felt keenly
aboard this ship. Since I had become quite intimate with
Bob, and therefore very fond of him I am conscious of a
personal loss.

Incidentally I am enclosing herewith a
postal money order in the amount of $18.82 which represents
the value of the Cigar Mess share held by Bob.

With sincere regards and fond hope that Bob
will turn up soon, I am

J. Flord Dreud
Chaplain U.S.N.

NT

NOV
27
1943

Letter from Bunker Hill Chaplain

Sherry Looking at Daddy Bob's Photo

After being notified by the Navy that Bob was missing in action, I can only imagine the anxiety that Ginny felt not knowing what had happened to the love of her life. Letters poured in from friends and relatives telling her to keep faith that Bob would turn up somewhere. There was nothing she could do but pray that he would be found safe and well. It was so far away. Her inability to do anything must have left her with a helpless feeling. She had one little girl, Sherry, and another on the way. She was faced with the fear of what the future held for her children and herself and how they would endure without Bob's love and support. Not knowing Bob's fate was almost worse than knowing if he was killed. Neither was good, but having some closure would have erased some of her anxiety. Living with her mother and father helped as she was not facing this terrible circumstance alone.

Ginny's strong faith was also a big help in allowing her to face each day. She was pregnant with her second child and had little Sherry who was less than a year old by her side. And while the war was still raged, the Allies were starting to get an upper hand. Ginny was not alone in facing the future without her husband. You couldn't go anywhere without seeing a parent, wife, or friend who had not lost someone they loved to this World War.

It was now 1944, and the United States had been fighting for three years and the rest of the world even longer. Industries in the States were manufacturing planes, guns, ammunition, as well as other war machines at a pace never before seen in history. Women had stepped up to fill jobs left open as more and more men left the U. S. to fight for their country. Japan and Germany had woken a "Sleeping Giant." Americans were determined that the war was going to be won by the Allies no matter what the cost.

The *Bunker Hill* continued to wage a successful war on Japan. The following places were all part of her history: Rabaul, The Gilberts, Nauru, KaviengI, II.III, The Marshalls, Truk, Caroline Islands, Tinian, Saipan, Marianas Islands, Hollandia, Guam, Battle of The Eastern Philippines, Pagan Island, Palau, Bonin Islands, Davao Area and Mindanao Central Philippines, Negros, Palau, Manila Area Philippines, Calamians, Philippines, Okinawa Shima Formosa, Luzon, Visayas, Ormolu Bay. Some of these areas were engaged more than once. The Bunker Hill and his crew did their part in the drive to Japan's main land.

(This was taken from The *Bunker Hill* Yearbook on the page called Roll of Honor of those who had died that year or were missing in action, R.H.Higley Lieutenant was one of them.)

Victory has its inevitable price. And never is there a time when the meaning of victory is more throughly felt than when its price includes the loss of human life. Someone gives his life so that someone else might survive; and that somebody who died might have been spared his fate one moment earlier. . . or one moment later.

The Grim Reaper moves upon the face of the Earth and its waters in a strange way. We never quite understand it; we're never quite ready to believe it. It's all a vague dream that happens to someone else we think.

Without exception the men who made the Supreme Sacrifice from the decks of the Bunker Hill, the roles of true shipmates, though they would have claimed to only be doing their job. They had given their time and talents to their country in a fight that promised to be long and hard; and in dying they gave their final energies, their everything, for a life they had hoped to retain in peace.

We salute those shipmates and, paying final tribute to them, we pledge our most intelligent powers to forbid their having died in vain.

The *Bunker Hill* continued its journey towards Japan as was reported earlier. When it reached the island of Okinawa the fighting was some of the worst of the war on the island. Nearly as many men were killed in taking the island (total from both sides) than died from the atomic bombs dropped later in Japan. The *Bunker Hill* was there for support from the air as well as to protect our troops from Japanese fighter planes and bombers. The Japanese were becoming

90

desperate and pilots were told that they would be rewarded both as heroes in this life and eternal rewards in the after life by purposely crashing their planes into our ships. Two Japanese kamikaze pilots did just that to the *Bunker Hill* on May 11,1945. They both flew their planes, loaded with 500 lb bombs, directly into the deck of the *Bunker Hill*, penetrating the flight deck. The bombs exploded below deck killing close to four hundred sailers and injuring many more. Other ships were used to take the injured and dead off the burning ship. The *Bunker Hill* was able to sail back to the US under its own power to be repaired. After being repaired it was used for bringing soldiers home, for training and finally as a communication platform until in 1974 when it was scrapped.

Document for May 11th:
"USS *Bunker Hill* hit by two Kamikazes in 30 seconds on 11 May 1945 off Kyushu."

"USS BUNKER HILL hit by two Kamikazes in 30 seconds on 11 May 1945 off Kyushu. Dead-372. Wounded-264."

"USS BUNKER HILL hit by two Kamikazes in 30 seconds on 11 May 1945 off Kyushu. Dead-372. Wounded-264." (National Archives Identifier: 520678); NWDNS-80-G-323712; General Photographic File of the Department of Navy, 1943 - 1958; General Records of the Department of the Navy, 1804 - 1958; Record Group 80; National Archives.

Taken on May 11, 1945, this photo shows the aircraft carrier USS *Bunker Hill* burning after being hit by two Japanese kamikaze attacks during the Battle of Okinawa.
More World War II Naval Photos...

Share, comment and suggest new documents at the Today's Document Tumblr Blog

Get the Today's Document RSS Feed RSS FEED | About RSS

Kamikaze's hit Bunker Hill

Lt. Bob's Navy Photo

THE SECRETARY OF THE NAVY

WASHINGTON

The President of the United States takes pleasure in presenting the DISTINGUISHED FLYING CROSS to

LIEUTENANT ROBERT H. HIGLEY, UNITED STATES NAVY

for service as set forth in the following

CITATION:

"For heroism and extraordinary achievement while participating in aerial flight as Pilot of a Torpedo Bomber attached to Torpedo Bombing Squadron SEVENTEEN in combat against enemy Japanese surface forces at Rabaul, New Britain, November 11, 1943. Although separated from other planes of his squadron, Lieutenant Higley valiantly pressed home his attack against a heavy Japanese warship despite violent fighter opposition and severe antiaircraft fire from enemy shore batteries and combatant vessels. His extreme courage in the face of grave danger and his unswerving devotion to duty contributed materially to the success of the engagement and were in keeping with the highest traditions of the United States Naval Service."

For the President,

James Forrestal

Secretary of the Navy

Letter from Secretary of Navy Awarding
Distinguished Flying Cross to Bob

94

The Distinguished Flying Cross

"FOR unswerving devotion to duty . . ." So reads the Distinguished Flying Cross citation of Lieutenant Charles A. McKinney, listed as missing in action with his gallant crew.

McKinney was the pilot of an Army B-25 during a perilously low-level bomb run over a Nazi convoy. As the bomber roared in at masthead level, a storm of antiaircraft fire raked the plane. Messerschmitt 109's dived in, desperately trying to save their supply ships. In a few seconds the B-25 was riddled by ack-ack, both engines crippled by a Nazi fighter's guns. McKinney could have jettisoned his bombs and made a crash landing.

But the B-25 never swerved. Holding to masthead height, McKinney headed straight across the convoy. When he banked away one Nazi ship was sinking, two more were damaged badly. The fury of the Nazi gunners was now concentrated on the crippled B-25, which exploded and fell into the sea.

The DFC was established on July 2, 1926. It is awarded to any member of the Army, Navy, Marine Corps or Coast Guard who has distinguished himself in aerial flight since April 6, 1917. The first award was made to Charles A. Lindbergh, after his flight to Paris. Other famous peacetime recipients include Glenn Curtiss, Admiral Byrd and Amelia Earhart.

High on the list of DFC heroes is Staff Sergeant James W. Kerns, from Elkins, West Virginia. Kerns was ball-turret gunner on a B-17 during action over Foggia Airdrome. Fierce enemy fighter attacks shattered his turret—how he escaped death is a mystery. Ordered into the radio room, Kerns was struck in the back by another exploding shell.

He was about to bandage his wound when he saw the tail gunner collapse, bleeding profusely. Carrying his comrade to a protected spot, Kerns manned the tail guns, driving off Nazi fighters. Then, returning to the injured gunner, he bandaged the man's wounds. By this time the B-17 was heading down for a crash landing in the sea. The safest position was to lie flat, but Kerns kept on his feet, tossing out all movable equipment which might hurtle forward and injure his comrades. He was still at it when the plane struck the water. Knocked unconscious, he was lifted into a raft by the crew.

On the Navy side, Lieutenant Ira Kepford stands at the top of DFC pilots with sixteen Jap planes to his credit. A member of the famous Skull and Crossbones squadron, Kepford once found himself and his squadron in a battle with more than a hundred Jap planes. In that furious melee, four Jap bombers went down before Kepford's guns and a fifth fled, severely damaged.

Typical of the devil-dog courage of Marine airmen was the singlehanded attack made by Lieutenant Robert M. Patterson on a Jap naval force. It was October 15, 1942, and the enemy was desperately attempting to reinforce his dwindling army on Guadalcanal. During the night a strong force, escorting crowded transports, had approached the island. Patterson took off in predawn darkness. Without even one supporting plane, he dived through heavy ack-ack from Jap ship and shore batteries, made a direct hit on a Jap transport. Returning for more bombs, he raced back, diving through fire from ten destroyers, and hit two more troopships, killing a large number of Japs.

Army, Navy or Marines, these are America's airmen—heroes of the sky who wear the DFC.

BY DONALD E. KEYHOE

A Silk moire ribbon—blue with white stripe near each edge and a narrow red center stripe outlined in white

B The medal is bronze, suspended from a bar to which the ribbon is attached

C Four-bladed propeller is superimposed on a bronze cross pattée

Service ribbon for lapel

* *

RECENT RECIPIENTS OF THE DISTINGUISHED FLYING CROSS

Lt. A. L. Jacobson, Navy
Tacoma, Washington

Capt. J. T. Godfrey
Woonsocket, R. I.

Maj. C. M. Kunz, USMC
Springfield, Missouri

NEXT MONTH: THE LEGION OF MERIT

D.F Cross Explanation

Southwest Pacific
17 January, 1944

My dear Ginny:

Every time we reach a place where we can get some mail we expect to have further news about Bob and his crew, but we still have no information. We have received nothing further on Bill Krantz and his crew since we heard that they were "in friendly hands" so we have concluded that they must be with some one of the many "coast-watchers", and there may be a long delay. Some few of these watchers have access to radio, but most of them are at isolated spots. In many cases rescued aviators live with them for 18 months or more before they can be reported safe. So we are still waiting for news of Bob -- as of course I know you are. He might possibly be able to communicate with you before we are notified so I would appreciate having any news you receive.

The enclosed check for $11 represents a sum of money we found in Bob's safe on the ship. I held it pending early news from him, but since you would probably see him before we do I am forwarding the check now.

You may have heard that Henry Carby and his crew have been missing since Christmas Day, and Grady Owens radioman was killed, another was wounded. This will indicate to you that we have been very busy, and in spite of our losses we have been extremely successful.

I wrote you a letter some time ago which I hear you had not received by 29 December. Also wrote to Bob's father and since you were reported to be on your way to Kansas City I presume that you have seen that letter.

The boys join me in sincere best wishes for a Happier New Year. I will continue to keep you posted.

Sincerely,

Frank

Letter From Frank to Ginny

Page 2

THE KAN

SON MISSING IN PACIF[

LIEUT. R. H. HIGLEY ON DUTY /
NAVAL FLIER.

Graduate of Junior College He
Was Awarded Silver Star for
Gallantry in the Casa-
blanca Landing.

Lieut. Robert Harrison Higley,
years old, was reported missing
action in the South Pacific by t
navy in a telegram today to h
parents, Mr. and Mrs. Harrison
Higley, 7015 Ward parkway.

He enlisted in 1939, took flig
training at Fairfax, Pensacola a
Miami, Fla., and was commission
August 2, 1941. He served on t
carrier Ranger more than two yea
Last April he was awarded the Silv
Star for participation in the Cas
blanca landing a year ago th
month. He recently had been
member of a torpedo squadron in t
South Pacific.

A graduate of Westport hi
school and Junior college, Lieute

MISSING IN ACTION IN THE SOUT
PACIFIC . . . LIEUT. ROBERT HAR
RISON HIGLEY.

ant Higley worked for the Standa
Milling company before his enlis
ment.

Lieutenant Higley's wife, Mrs. Vi
ginia Higley, and a daughter, Shar
Jean Higley, 9 months old, now a
with Mrs. Higley's parents, Cap
and Mrs. James M. Adam, at Gro
City, Pa., where Captain Adam
commanding officer of a marin
detachment. He also has a sist
Miss Virginia Higley, secretary
St. Andrew's Episcopal church.

Kansas City Star Article of Bob Missing

COMBAT LOSS FORM
US Naval and Marine Corps aircraft combat losses
World War 2
from US Navy Records including
Bureau of Personnel, Casualty Section

DATE:	11 NOVEMBER 1943
AIRCRAFT:	TBF-1C AVENGER
SERIAL NUMBER:	24512
UNIT:	VT-17 (TORPEDO BOMBER SQUADRON 17)
SHIP:	USS BUNKER HILL
BASE:	USS BUNKER HILL
PILOT:	ROBERT H. HIGLEY,
SERIAL NUMBER:	NOT GIVEN
RANK:	LIEUTENANT USNR
CREW:	NOT GIVEN
LOCATION OF LOSS:	RABAUL
NOTES:	COMBAT MISSION, MISSING IN ACTION.
REMARKS:	SECOND RABAUL STRIKE (11 NOVEMBER 1943): TWO CARRIER TASK FORCES (REAR ADMIRALS F. C. SHERMAN AND A.E. MONTGOMERY, USS INDEPENDENCE) WITH THREE HEAVY AND TWO LIGHT CRUISERS HIT JAPANESE NAVAL SHIPPING AT RABAUL SINKING ONE DESTROYER AND DAMAGING TWO CRUISRS AND OTHER SHIPS. IN THIS ATTACK THE SB2C CURTISS HELLDIVER WAS USED IN COMBAT FOR THE FIRST TIME.

Combat Loss Form

Letters to be each on their own page with title below each one:

THE SECRETARY OF THE NAVY

WASHINGTON

4 December 1943

Mrs. Robert Harrison Higley
c/o Capt. J. M. Adams, USMCR
Marine Detachment
Grove City, Pennsylvania

Dear Mrs. Higley:

It was with deep regret that I learned that your
husband, Lieutenant Robert Harrison Higley, United
States Navy, has been missing in action since
11 November 1943 in the Atlantic area.

Public Law 490, as amended, makes certain provisions
for the support of dependents and the payment of
insurance premiums by allotments from the pay of
persons in a status similar to that of your husband.
For information or to make specific requests in
terms of need, it is suggested that you communicate with
the Chief of Naval Personnel, Navy Department.

I desire to extend my sincere sympathy to you in
your anxiety and it is hoped that you may find
comfort in the thought that your husband was
upholding the highest traditions of the Navy,
in the service of his country.

Sincerely yours,

Frank Knox

Secretary of the Navy

THE KANSAS CITY AREA COUNCIL

BOY SCOUTS OF AMERICA

LAND BANK BUILDING   **KANSAS CITY 6, MISSOURI**

OFFICE OF THE EXECUTIVE
H. ROE BARTLE

February 23, 1946

Mrs. Robert H. Higley
Misses Sharon Jean and Nancy Lynn
1288 West 71st Street Terrace
Kansas City 5, Missouri

My dear Mrs. Higley:

I know that your heart must have suffered the depths of
sorrow during these last weeks, in receiving the official
notice that our Lieutenant must be "presumed to be dead"
after his illustrious service and the long months of MIA.
It goes without saying that you have had high courage and
strength during the darkest hours, for with two sweet girlies
by your side much has been required of you for their sakes
as well as for Bob's. Surely he would want you to carry on
for him .. and I am sure that if he could be with you in person
as well as in spirit he would speak his pride in your courage
and steadfastness. Our thoughts and prayers have been with you
often in the difficult days though you have passed, and we will
continue to pray that strength and courage and the peace that
passeth all understanding will be yours.

Bob's Scouting brothers will ever hold his memory in reverence
.. and if there is any way in which we may serve you, you
have but to command.

May the Great Scoutmaster be with you always.

Faithfully yours,

H. Roe Bartle
Scout Executive

HRB:H

NAVY DEPARTMENT

Pers-5323a-rra   **BUREAU OF NAVAL PERSONNEL**
98687   WASHINGTON 25, D. C.

MAR 1 4 1945

Mrs. Virginia A. Higley
c/o Capt. J. M. Adam
Marine Detachment
Grove City, Pennsylvania

In Re: Lieutenant Robert H. Higley, USN

Dear Mrs. Higley:

Realizing that the naval service of the above-named officer
must be a source of pride to you, a copy of the synopsis of his
record, compiled by the Bureau, is herewith enclosed.

This synopsis will be of help to you in filling out applications
for benefits. Upon request, the Bureau will be glad to furnish
additional data from the files to assist you.

By direction of Chief of Naval Personnel.

                                   Sincerely yours,

                                   H. B. ATKINSON
                                   Commander, USNR
                                   Officer in Charge
                                   Casualty Section

Encl.

In reply address not the signer of this
letter, but Bureau of Naval Personnel,
Navy Department, Washington 25, D.C.

Refer to No.

Pers-5323a-rra
98687   MAR 1 4 1945

NAVY DEPARTMENT

BUREAU OF NAVAL PERSONNEL

WASHINGTON 25, D. C.

LIEUTENANT ROBERT HARRISON HIGLEY, U. S. NAVY, ACTIVE, DECEASED

Re: Service of

1917 Jun 8 Born in Ancon, Canal Zone.

U. S. ARMY SERVICE

Enlisted			Discharged		
1934 Oct 4			1937 Oct 3		

ENLISTED SERVICE

1940 Sep 24		1941 Jan 26	To accept appointment as Aviation Cadet, USNR.

OFFICER SERVICE

1941 Jan 21 Appointed Aviation Cadet, U. S. Naval Reserve, to rank from 15 January 1941.

Jan 21 Ordered to Naval Air Station, Pensacola, Florida, for active duty undergoing training. Reported 27 January 1941. Detached 20 June 1941.

Jan 27 Accepted appointment and executed oath of office as Aviation Cadet.

Jun 6 Ordered to Naval Air Station, Miami, Florida, for active duty undergoing training. Reported 23 June 1941. Detached 4 August 1941.

Jul 10 Designated Naval Aviator (Heavier-than-Air).

Jul 24 Commissioned regular Ensign, A-V(N), U. S. Naval Reserve, to rank from 21 June 1941.

Aug 2 Ordered to Fleet Air Detachment, Naval Air Station, Norfolk, Virginia, for temporary duty involving flying under training. Reported 24 August 1941. Detached 30 September 1941.

Aug 2 Ordered to USS RANGER, Scouting Squadron FORTY-ONE for duty involving flying. Reported 30 September 1941. Detached 30 January 1943.

Aug 4 Accepted appointment and executed oath of office as Ensign, A-V(N), U. S. Naval Reserve.

1942 Jun 16 Accepted appointment and executed oath of office as Lieutenant (junior grade), A-V(N), to rank from 15 June 1942. Alnav 120-42.

1943 Jan 28 Ordered to Torpedo Squadron SEVENTEEN for duty involving flying.

Mar 1 Appointed Lieutenant, A-V(N), U. S. Naval Reserve, for temporary service to rank from 1 March 1943. Alnav 37-43.

-1-

102

1943 Jun 20 Commission in U. S. Naval Reserve terminated this date to
               accept appointment in U. S. Navy.

1943 Jun 10 Commissioned Ensign, regular, U. S. Navy, from 21 June 1941.
      Jun 21 Accepted appointment and executed oath of office.
      Jun 21 Appointed Lieutenant for temporary service to rank from
               1 March 1943. Transmittal letter, dated 10 June 1943.

               MEDALS: PURPLE HEART
                              SILVER STAR MEDAL
                              DISTINGUISHED FLYING CROSS
                              American Defense Service Medal (Bronze "A")
                              World War II Victory Medal
                              European-African-Middle-Eastern Area Campaign
                                              Medal - One (1) bronze star
                              Asiatic-Pacific Area Campaign Medal - One (1)
                                                        bronze star

               Died: Presumptive - 11 January 1946. Officially
                              determined to be MISSING IN ACTION as of
                              11 November 1943, when the plane in which
                              he was flying, a unit of Torpedo Squadron
                              SEVENTEEN, based aboard the USS BUNKER HILL,
                              failed to return from a strike against
                              enemy vessels in the Rabaul Area. In
                              compliance with Section 5 of Public Law 490,
                              as amended, death is presumed to have occurred
                              on the 11th day of January 1946.

               Place: Rabaul Area (Pacific Area)

               Cause: Plane failed to return from strike against
                              enemy vessels. (Enemy Action)

               Next of Kin: Virginia Adam Higley, Wife
                              % Capt. J. M. Adam
                              Marine Detachment
                              Grove City, Pennsylvania

NAVY DEPARTMENT

BUREAU OF NAVAL PERSONNEL.

WASHINGTON 25, D. C.

3 May 1946

Mrs. Virginia A. Higley,
c/o Captain J. M. Adam,
Marine Detachment,
Grove City, Pennsylvania.

Dear Mrs. Higley:

The Bureau has the honor to inform you of the award of the Purple Heart and certificate to your late husband,

LIEUTENANT ROBERT H. HIGLEY, U. S. NAVY

in accordance with General Order 186 of January 21, 1943 which reads in part as follows:

"The Secretary of the Navy is further authorized and directed to award the Purple Heart posthumously, in the name of the President of the United States, to any persons who, while serving in any capacity with the Navy, Marine Corps or Coast Guard of the United States, since December 6, 1941, are killed in action or who die as a direct result of wounds received in action with an enemy of the United States, or as a result of an act of such enemy."

The medal is being forwarded under separate cover. Please acknowledge receipt on the enclosed form.

By direction of the Chief of Naval Personnel.

Sincerely yours,

L. C. Thompson,
Lieutenant Commander, U.S.N.R.,
Medals and Awards.

Enclosures

Purple Heart Letter

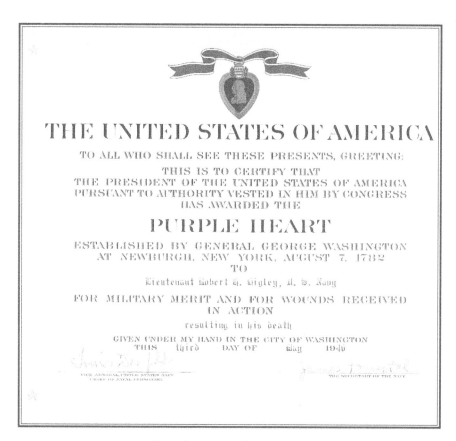

Purple Heart Certificate

Navy Wings, WWII Medal, European African
Middle Eastern Medal, Silver Star Medal

WWII Medals, Asiatic Pacific Campaign, American Defense
Distinguished Flying Cross and Purple Heart

IN GRATEFUL MEMORY OF

Robert H. Higley

WHO DIED IN THE SERVICE OF HIS COUNTRY

attached to Torpedo Squadron 17, Pacific Area, 11 January 1946 (Presumed)

HE STANDS IN THE UNBROKEN LINE OF PATRIOTS WHO HAVE DARED TO DIE

THAT FREEDOM MIGHT LIVE, AND GROW, AND INCREASE ITS BLESSINGS.

FREEDOM LIVES, AND THROUGH IT, HE LIVES—

IN A WAY THAT HUMBLES THE UNDERTAKINGS OF MOST MEN

Harry Truman

PRESIDENT OF THE UNITED STATES OF AMERICA

President Truman Letter

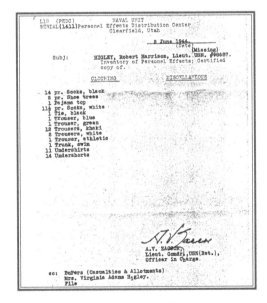

```
L19 (PEDC)              NAVAL UNIT
SERIAL(1411)Personal Effects Distribution Center
                        Clearfield, Utah
                        2 June 1944.
                        (Date)
                        (Missing)
Subj:           HIGLEY, Robert Harrison, Lieut., USN. #98687
                Inventory of Personal Effects; Certified
                copy of.

        1.      An inventory of the subject's personal ef-
fects was held this date and consists of the following
items as listed hereon.  These effects have been turned
over to the Supply Officer for shipment to next of kin,
Mrs. Virginia Adams Higley, (Wife)
1288 W. 71st Terrace, Kansas City, Missouri.

        CLOTHING                    MISCELLANEOUS

1 Belt, leather             2 Books, religious
1 Cap, officer, complete    2 Brushes, hair
1 Cap, overseas, green      4 Balls, golf
2 Caps, overseas, khaki     1 Bag, golf
1 Cap, aviators             13 Clubs, golf
1 Capcover, blue            1 Kit, sewing
1 Capcover, green           1 Kit, containing: (19 U.S. coins,
1 Capcover, white             4 Foreign coins, 1 money belt,
1 Coat, blue                  2 Navy wings, large, 1 Navy wings
1 Coat, green                 small, 2 shoulder boards, 2 colla:
2 Coats, khaki                bars, 1 sweetheart pin, 2 campaig:
2 Coats, white                bars, 1 identification bracelet
1 pr. Gloves, suede           1 sterling napkin holder,
1 pr. Gloves, cotton          1 fountain pen "Parker", 1 case,
10 Handkerchiefs              jewelry, containing: 1 pr cuff
1 Jersey, athletic            links, 2 collar buttons, 2 reli-
2 Jerseys, sport              gious medals, 1 pr. baby boots,
3 pr. Pajamas                 1 Electric razor, "Shavemaster",
10 Shirts, khaki              1 Naval certificate, (Aviators),
2 Shirts, white               1 billfold, 37 snapshots,
1 pr. Shoes, brown, low       3 snapshots, cases)
1 pr. Shoes, white, low     1 New Testament
1 pr. Slippers, house       3 Photos, frame
1 pr. Sneakers
```

Clothes List of Items sent back to Ginny

```
L19 (PEDC)              NAVAL UNIT
SERIAL(1411)Personal Effects Distribution Center
                        Clearfield, Utah
                        2 June 1944.
                        (Date)
                        (Missing)
Subj:           HIGLEY, Robert Harrison, Lieut. USN. #98687.
                Inventory of Personal Effects; Certified
                copy of.

        CLOTHING                    MISCELLANEOUS

14 pr. Socks, black
2 pr. Shoe trees
1 Pajama top
11½ pr. Socks, white
1 Tie, black
1 Trouser, blue
1 Trouser, green
12 Trousers, khaki
2 Trousers, white
1 Trouser, athletic
1 Trunk, swim
11 Undershirts
14 Undershorts




                        A.V. ZAGGOR,
                        Lieut. Comdr., USN(Ret.),
                        Officer in Charge.

cc:  BuPers (Casualties & Allotments)
     Mrs. Virginia Adams Higley.
     File
```

Continue list of Clothes

CARRIER AIR GROUP SEVENTEEN

c/o Fleet Post Office
San Francisco, California
29 December 1943

Dear Mrs. Higley,

        I received your letter and I know how you must feel. I am very sorry we had to report "Hig" missing but don't give up hope. I can assure you that to the best of our knowledge there is every possibility that he may be in friendly hands.

        I regret that I cannot give you any specific details as to location or mission. I understand that "Frank" his skipper has already written to you. You may rest assured that the mission he was on with us was very successful and he did his full share.

        We, all of us, are still expecting to hear about his return and we don't intend to give up hope, for we firmly believe that old "Hig" will show up one of these days. So hold up your chin.

        With best wishes and a sincere hope that the New Year will be good to you and yours.

Sincerely,

Bog

Comdr. M.P.Bagdanovich, USN.
Commander, Carrier Air Group SEVENTEEN

Mrs. R.H.Higley
Marine Detachment
Grove City, Pa.

CARRIER GROUP 17 LETTER From
Commander M. P. Bagdanovich

My dear Ginny:

Now that we are in from a very long cruise at sea, almost two months, I can at last write you what we know of Bob's accident. Your letter was waiting when we arrived and I know that you must feel that we had deserted you, when as a matter of fact it has not been possible for us to get any mail off before now. Then too, for security reasons it was impossible to write immediately since I did not want to risk anything that might lessen Bob's chances of being picked up -- information concerning possible survivors from water crashes is closely guarded for obvious reasons. Let me tell you as much of the story as I can. You will of course treat this information as confidential -- and for this reason I am censoring this letter myself, and writing you this personal letter instead of an official one.

Bob went with us on the attack on Rabaul on the 11th of November. We had a rather rough time of it as the Japs were out in force to intercept the attack. My squadron attacked several big Jap ships and enemy fighters were all over the sky. In the heat of the battle very few pilots were able to take notice of any planes but their own until we were on the way back to the ship. Planes joined up whenever they fell in with one of our own, and we returned in groups. On this account none of us knew until we got back aboard whether everyone had been accounted for. Henry Carby was the last to return, long after the others, having had a running fight with some zeros for many miles. Dickson reported that Bill Krantz made a forced landing in the water and that all three men were seen in their rubber boat --not too far from an island where there were some of our own forces. We waited for Bob, but he did not return. None of the pilots in the entire group saw him go down or had any reason to think he was in trouble. I can only give you my own opinion of what must have happened, Ginny --an opinion formed after talking with everyone who could add anything worthwhile.

Since we did not see Bob get hit by AA fire --as Bill Krantz' plane was -- and since no one actually saw him go into the water it is my belief that his plane was either shot down by enemy fighters, or he made a forced landing in the water. In either case I have every reason to believe that he may have been able to make his way to land in his rubber boat with his crew. Depending on where he went down, the chances of his being taken prisoner cannot be established, though knowing Bob and the two excellent men who were with him I cannot believe that they would have put ashore in enemy-held territory.,If they were able to make a safe water landing and get ashore on one of the many islands it could very well be six months or more before they

110

are able to contact our own forces. There have been many instances of such rescues, though all of us have been expecting daily to hear from him.

When it became apparent that Bob would not return to the ship we sent despatches to all activities which could be of assistance in effecting a rescue. I had this repeated from the Flagship two days later so there could be no mistake. Upon arriving here I sent despatches to the Commander in Chief of the Pacific Fleet, to Admiral Halsey, and to the Commander in the Solomons area requesting information on Bob and Krantz. I have not had time to receive replies, but I didn't want to delay this letter until they are answered. You may be sure that I will leave nothing undone which might be of any help to Bob -- and you will be immediately informed of anything we are able to learn. The Navy has a very complete rescue service in all these areas. We have personally contacted all of them to make sure that there can be no mistakes. That we have heard nothing from either Bob or Bill Krantz after five weeks is not indicative of anything because the area where they went down is very difficult to reach. All of the natives in these areas are freindly to our own forces, so they may be counted upon to be helpful. Bob had sufficient equipment to take care of himself, and he knew how to use it. His was one of the best flight teams in the squadron, as you know.

I as well as all of my boys have every confidence that Bob will turn up somewhere one of these days, or we will at least hear from him. I do not want to have you build up false hopes any more than I want to suggest a pessimistic view. Your own confidence in Bob, and the fact that he had already seen combat duty is a strong argument in favor of the thought that he would be able to bring himself and his crew out of a tight spot.

We have packed Bob's gear for shipment to you since he would undoubtedly be sent home after being found. He had a small amount of cash in his safe which I will forward to you by my personal check to save time.

Ginny, you must know that I am deeply concerned about Bob, as I would be about any of my boys -- but in the last few months I have spent a lot of my leisure time with Bob and as you know we had become very good friends. On this account I have written exactly what I think and feel about Bob's chances -- because I want you to know. Please feel free to write me about anything, especially if I may be able to help you in any way. I am writing to your father tonight. All of the boys join me in hoping for the best, with God's help.

Most sincerely,

Frank

Westport High School

has inscribed on its

Roll of Honor

the name of

Robert Higley

who made the supreme sacrifice

in World War II

∽∾ ∽∾ ∽∾

Dulce et decorum est pro patria mori.—Horace

A sweet and beautiful thing
it is to die for one's country

High School Roll of Honor

D'ARCY ADVERTISING COMPANY
INCORPORATED
MISSOURI   PACIFIC   BUILDING
SAINT LOUIS
OFFICES - - - NEW YORK · CLEVELAND · ATLANTA · TORONTO

NEW YORK OFFICE
515 MADISON AVE.
TEL. PLAZA 8-2600
Ex 35

Home —
159 E. 49th St.
New York, N.Y.
C/o B. Kuse
Tel. ELDORADO-5-1670
November 24, 1943

Dear Ginny,

    I just heard the news of Bob's being among the missing. Ginny,
Bill is missing too and I know just what you are going through.....
    Hope is the essential thing now and faith in God that all will
be ok soon and that they will turn up so- fat,well and happy.
    I have been to numerous people that have influence in Washington
and they are doing all they can to help. Also this firm I am working
for sponsers Radio programs and have offered to put me on their
next prisoner program. That is the type of thing, that they have
the families of missing boys,whom they are pretty sure are prisoners
of war, speak in hopes that they will be among those that hear the
broadcast,and know that everything is all right.
    Everyone has been so kind to me and have tried to make it much
easier. As yet, I'm in a sort of daze and don't realize too much about
things. You see I came in on Wed. 17th and when I got into the apartment
Barb broke the news which had just been relayed to her. It seemed to
me that I had heard someone, somewhere, before saying just the words
she said, or that it was just a bad dream.. But Ginny, I never will
give up hope. Bill and Bob are as much in love with us as we are with
them, and I know that they want to come back and feel that they have a
lot to live for, so if there is any way that they can possibly get
word to us they will.
    The last letter that I received from Bill was the 7th of Nov. He had
just gone to confession and received commien. communion. He said that
he was going into the real thing within a few moments after writing the
letter and that,if anything happened to him, not to give up hope.
    This has been doubly hard for me to keep my chin up Ginny, cause I
just lost my baby, and it naturally was pretty hard for me to take...
Both things so precious to me. But I have put my faith in God and know
that Bill will be turning up some one of these days and be proud of me,
going on just as he would want me to...
    My job of Secretary to th Personal Manager of D'Arcy's is wonderful/
I live with 4 grand girls but am soon to take an apartment with Vee Kridel.
    Please write me soon Ginny, at this address or at my home address. If
you ever wish to do so, you may call me at either no. I don't work Sat.
at all, so if you ever wish to see me on any weekend, let me know. I
believe you are quite near.......
    Love to you and Sherry, Keep your chin up and pray as you have

never prayed before.   When I make Novena Mon.   I will light a

candle for BOB also.

P.S. Excuse letter. Been
between hops etc - - -

Love
Fran

D'Arcy Advertising Letter from Friend to Ginny

Southwest Pacific
17 January, 1944

My dear Ginny:

Every time we reach a place where we can get some mail we expect to have further news about Bob and his crew, but we still have no information. We have received nothing further on Bill Krantz and his crew since we heard that they were "in friendly hands" so we have concluded that they must be with some one of the many "coast-watchers", and there may be a long delay. Some few of these watchers have access to radio, but most of them are at isolated spots. In many cases rescued aviators live with them for 10 months or more before they can be reported safe. So we are still waiting for news of Bob -- as of course I know you are. He might possibly be able to communicate with you before we are notified so I would appreciate having any news you receive.

The enclosed check for $11 represents a sum of money we found in Bob's safe on the ship. I held it pending early news from him, but since you would probably see him before we do I am forwarding the check now.

You may have heard that Henry Carby and his crew have been missing since Christmas Day, and Grady Owens radioman was killed, another was wounded. This will indicate to you that we have been very busy, and in spite of our losses we have been extremely successful.

I wrote you a letter some time ago which I hear you had not received by 29 December. Also wrote to Bob's father and since you were reported to be on your way to Kansas City I presume that you have seen that letter.

The boys join me in sincere best wishes for a Happier New Year. I will continue to keep you posted.

Sincerely,

Frank

January 17, 1944 letter from Frank

BACK TO KANSAS CITY, MISSOURI

Not long after Bob was reported "missing in action," Ginny and Sherry moved back to Kansas City, Missouri, to live with her parents. Mail was forwarded to her, by military coordinators, from many friends that wanted to show her support.

Nancy Lynn Higley is born.

Ginny was sad and worried about Bob, but she was also about to have her second child. It was now February 1944 and her second child was due soon. Ginny was still living with her parents in Kansas City when she went into labor. Another little girl was born February 20,1944, 8 lbs. 4oz. and named Nancy Lynn Higley. Bob would have been so proud if he could have been there. Ginny now had the joy of two daughters and also the responsibility. Ginny's mother Ruth was a God send and became a very important figure in both Sherry's and Nancy's lives. James Adam was still serving in the Marine Corps for his second tour of duty. Ginny did just what she had done for all of her keep-sakes with Bob, and saved every little thing of the girls. She had congratulation cards, gift lists, birthday cards and lots of photos.

Ginny's mother, Ruth, had started a "cottage industry" in her basement to help wives of service men keep busy. This came about in an unusual way. Ruth Adam and her daughter, Ginny, had been living on the East Coast when Bob was reported missing at Rabaul. Ruth's husband was still serving in the Marine Corps. They moved back to Kansas City, Missouri, in late 1943. Ruth had taught Ginny how to knit to help take her mind off of what may have happened to Bob. In October of 1944, Ginny made some soakers (knit bottoms for Babies) for presents to Navy wives. Ruth helped decorate them. One day when Ruth was going to the Post Office she stopped at one of her favorite stores, Harzfelds of Kansas City. The clerk wanted to know what Ruth was mailing and she showed her the cute baby bottoms. The clerk showed them to the store's buyer, a lady by the name Mrs. Muriel Crowley. Mrs. Crowley asked if Ruth could have three dozen made up because the store was short of Christmas merchandise. Ruth and Ginny filled the order. Ruth decided to call other stores in several cities to see if they would be interested in similar items. She called her sister-in-law, Mrs R.W. Couffer, in Chicago and asked if she could make some contacts for her.

Ruth said, at the time, "I had no background in business. I had been a teacher in Chicago and Detroit, before my marriage." Ruth asked other ladies in her neighborhood if they would like to make extra money knitting, and they started making items for the new company she named "Personality Incorporated." The little company grew and at its peak sold to stores all across the country including Marshall Fields, Neiman Marcus, Saks and many others. Her business not only filled a need for wartime wives but also created wonderful handmade unique gifts for new borns. Ruth also went on to write a children's book teaching children about good manners and proper conduct called, *Personality Tales.*

The year was now 1945 and people were in a war nearing its end. Ginny still had some hope that Bob would be found but it was growing dimmer. Bob Higley's legacy continues in those he left behind, his wife and daughters and their families. Sherry and Nancy were brought up by Ginny as well as their Grandmother Ruth, later to be called Gran and then GiGi. Grandpa James, was there too as a father figure. Sherry and Nancy were given a great deal of love by their mother as well as their grandparents. James Adam was not with them too long as he started having what he thought were back problems but was then diagnosed as pancreatic cancer. He died at the age of 55 and Ruth's business became even more important after his death to help her financially. Bob's mother, Mayme, had also lost her husband when he was in his 50's, and her daughter Virginia, was diagnosed with multiple sclerosis. They were encouraged by doctors at that time, to move to Portland, Oregon, for more help with the disease.

Baby Nancy Higley

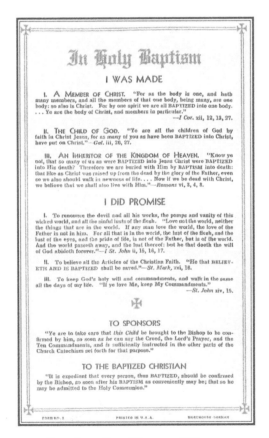

Baptism Certificate of Nancy

Photo of Ginny, Nancy and Sherry on Stairs

119

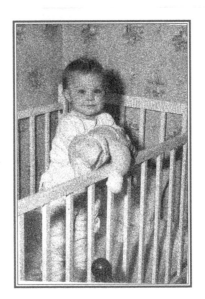

Nancy in Crib

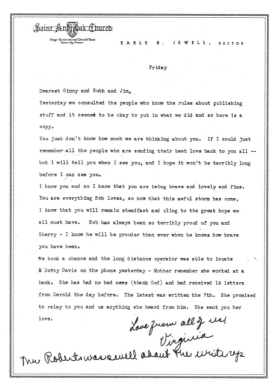

Saint Andrews Church

EARLE B. JEWELL, RECTOR

Friday

Dearest Ginny and Ruth and Jim,

Yesterday we consulted the people who know the rules about publishing stuff and it seemed to be okay to put in what we did and so here is a copy.

You just don't know how much we are thinking about you. If I could just remember all the people who are sending their best loves back to you all -- but I will tell you when I see you, and I hope it won't be terribly long before I can see you.

I know you and so I know that you are being brave and lovely and fine. You are everything Bob loves, so now that this awful storm has come, I know that you will remain steadfast and cling to the great hope we all must have. Bob has always been so terribly proud of you and Sherry - I know he will be prouder than ever when he knows how brave you have been.

We took a chance and the long distance operator was able to locate R Dotty Davis on the phone yesterday - Mother remember she worked at a bank. She has had no bad news (thank God) and had received 14 letters from Derold the day before. The latest was written the 7th. She promised to relay to you and us anything she heard from him. She sent you her love.

Love from all of us
Virginia

Mrs Roberts was swell about the write up

Letter from Saint Andrews Church

Nancy with Hair Ribbon

Virginia, Sherry and Nancy with Bob's Photo Behind

Sherry and Nancy

Navy Department, Washington 25, D. C.
Refer to No.

NAVY DEPARTMENT
BUREAU OF NAVAL PERSONNEL
WASHINGTON 25, D. C.

Pers-10/lw
98687

19 August 1948

Mrs. Robert H. Higley
1288 West 71 Terrace
Kansas City 5, Missouri

Dear Mrs. Higley:

The Chief of Naval Personnel has the honor to forward herewith the awards of the Asiatic-Pacific Campaign Medal and European-African-Middle Eastern Campaign Medal made posthumously to your husband, the late Robert H. Higley, United States Navy.

In order that you may understand the significance of the above awards there is enclosed a bulletin which sets forth the regulations governing their issuance.

By direction of Chief of Naval Personnel:

Sincerely yours,

M. Lanham

M. LANHAM
LTJG, USN
Medals and Awards

Encls-3

Aug. 19 Letter Award Asiatic-Pacific Medal and European-African-Middle East Medal

Photo of Sherry

Photo of Nancy

Jean Adam, Virginia's sister married Marvin Small, who was in the Army Air Corps during the war, and they had two daughters, Susan and Diane. The four girls, Sherry, Nancy, Susan and Diane became very close as they were taken to Lake Geneva, Wisconsin, each summer by their grandmother, Ruth. She would take the four girls to the lake to visit her brother Bob and his wife Fran. They learned to swim, water ski and create great memories.

The girls were all about one year apart in stair steps with Sherry the oldest, then Nancy followed by Susan and Diane. Jean and Marvin later had an age split family with two more children born later in their marriage, Trey and Debra.

Four Cousins: Sherry, Nancy, Susan and Diane
at Lake Geneva, Wisconsin (Circa 1950)

Nancy and Sherry Ballet

Picture of Nancy

Sherry and Nancy with Teddy Bear

Sherry, Ginny and Nancy

Sherry, Ruth, Ginny and Nancy

John & Virginia Pennington, Sherry, Nancy,
Jimmy, Johnny and Gail (Circa 1960)

This book was written to honor Bob Higley, but also to tell a little bit of his legacy that he was not able to enjoy. Biographies of Sherry and Nancy are not written, but a short version of their lives is included. They both grew up in Kansas City, Missouri. They took dancing and even started their own small dance studio, where they taught children. Ginny met and married John Pennington, also a pilot, when the girls were about nine and ten. They had three children together, Jimmy, Johnny and Gail. This made for a lively and fun filled household with the three younger siblings. Sherry graduated from Shawnee Mission East High School in Kansas City. John Pennington flew for Braniff Airlines and was transferred to Dallas, Texas in 1962, where Braniff's Headquarters were located. Nancy graduated from Richardson High School, in Richardson, Texas.

Sherry enrolled in college at Texas Christian University in Fort Worth, Texas, and then transferred to The University of Oklahoma. She met John Wasserburger in Kansas City while visiting her Grandmother Ruth, and they fell in love. They were married in Fort Leavenworth, Kansas in a traditional military service, where John was stationed. They had four children, Robby, Ricky, Ann, and Michael.

John served in the US Army and two tours of duty in Vietnam. John and Sherry and family moved to San Diego, California in1981. John retired after twenty years in the Army as a Lieutenant Colonel.

The Best Thing Thing That Ever Happened To Me

Nancy also went to Texas Christian University. She became a Pi Phi just like her mother and sister. In 1966 Nancy was waiting for a standby flight from Love Field Airport in Dallas, Texas, to visit her grandmother, Ruth, in Kansas City for the Easter Break. I was also a TCU student waiting for a half price flight by "student standby" to fly back to Iowa for Easter. We missed several flights from Love Field in Dallas and noticed each other each time. I finally asked her if she would like to get something to eat. We became acquainted and finally got on a flight north. Nancy's grandmother met her at the gate in Kansas City (when that was allowed) I was introduced to her Grandmother Ruth. After I left she said to Nancy, "Why don't you date a nice boy like Jim?" When we returned to TCU following Easter break, I received a call from Nancy asking me to go to the Pi Beta Phi formal. I accepted and we started dating.

In 1966 I left TCU and joined the Marine Corps Reserve for six months active duty and six years in the reserve. We were married in 1968 and celebrated our 50th anniversary on June 1, 2018. (The story of our courtship appeared in the TCU Magazine Winter Edition 2019, "Stories of How I met my Spouse at TCU.") The first summer after we started dating, Nancy invited me to go with her to Lake Geneva, Wisconsin to spend a few days and to meet her relatives, the Couffer Family. She had asked them if this would be alright and they said yes. What wonderful hosts they were. We became friends and have been invited back now for over 50 years to ski, swim, play tennis and enjoy each other's company.

We have a daughter, Alison Grabau Pomerantz, son-In-Law, Dr. Ben Pomerantz, as well as their daughters Morgan and Mackenzie. We also have a son Ryan, daughter-in-law Andrea, and their children Sam, Sophie and Will. We have been blessed with a wonderful family and five fantastic grandchildren. I often tell Nancy that I am very thankful to her father for his gift to me, she is the "best thing that ever happened to me".

Epworth Hi-Lights

Pictured are Misses Sherry and Nancy Higley and Susan and Diane Small, known as the "Talent Scouts," who will feature their pupils in ballet, toe, acrobatics, baton, tap and modern jazz in their presentation, "Epworth Hi-Lights," at Epworth Auditorium at 8 p.m. tonight. The four are graduates of Flaugh-Lewis School of ... Dance in Kansas City. — (Daily News Photo)

Four Cousins in Dance Show

Sherry and Nancy Early Twenties

Sherry Higley and John Wasserburger Wedding (circa 1965)

John Pennington, Nancy Higley Grabau, Jim Grabau
and Virginia Pennington (circa 1968)

Diane Wells, Susan Small, Gail Pennington, Nancy,
Jim Grabau, Jim-Jim Munson, Emily
Munson, Peggy Yochem and Barbra Glew, Wedding Party

Jim & Nancy Grabau Honey Moon Acapulco, Mexico

Pennington Family, John and Virginia, Gail, Jimmy and Johnny

Nancy with Ruth (Gigi) Adam

Nancy and Jim Grabau Home in Boone, Iowa

John & Sherry Wasserburger, Jim & Nancy Grabau (Circa 1970)

Children: Robby, Ricky, Ann and Michael Wasserburger,
Alison and Ryan Grabau (Circa 1975)

Ryan and Alison Grabau (circa 1974)

Couffer Family at Lake Geneva, Wisconsin

Nancy Grabau at Lake Geneva

Jim and Nancy at Lake Geneva, Wisconsin (Circa 2016)

Jim and Nancy Grabau, Alison Pomerantz,
Andrea, Ryan Grabau (Circa 2003)

John Pennington Jr., Sherry Wasserburger, Nancy Grabau, Virginia
Pennington, Gail Crutchfield, Dr. Jim Pennington (Circa 2003)

Three Sisters, Sherry Wasserburger, Nancy
Grabau and Gail Crutchfield

Buddy and Gail Crutchfield, Nancy and Jim Grabau

Dr. Ben and Alison Pomerantz, Morgan and Mackenzie

Grabau and Pomerantz Families at 50th Lake
Geneva, Wisconsin and Family (Circa 2018)

Jim, Nancy Grabau, Morgan and Mackenzie Pomerantz

JIM & NANCY'S 50TH ANNIVERSARY
LAKE GENEVA, WISCONSIN

Jim and Nancy Grabau 50th Wedding Anniversary Cruise

Virginia and Alison Grabau Pomerantz

Family Reunion San Diego, California (Circa 2018)

Dr. Jim Pennington and Wife Leslie

When Virginia passed her son Dr. Jim Pennington gave a eulogy for her funeral at the Episcopal Church of The Transfiguration in Dallas, Texas. I was trained as a "tough Marine" but I still get tears running down my cheeks when I read it. Because it was so well written, I have chosen to keep it in its entirety. It also pays tribute to Virginia's courage and zest for life.

Memorial Service, January 19, 2015 Eulogy by Dr. Jim Pennington

I owe a lot, if not the most of who I am to my mom. I know this because my kids are constantly saying, "There's Dad being Nana." I used to get defensive about this, but years ago I decided this was something I was proud of. Whenever I'm doing holiday traditions or taking too many family pictures, I'm" being Nana". I'm proud because she devoted her entire life to her family.

When my older sisters, Sherry and Nancy were teens, Mother ran a dance studio in the basement of our Kansas City home. Sherry and Nancy taught the classes, but Mother did the rest— the PR, the business, writing scripts for the shows and emceeing the shows for hundreds of students. How did she do this with three smaller children in tow?! (As a parent I could barely get my teens to apply their acne cream' much less teach dance lessons.)

She not only sent me with lunch to school, but had cut the crust off the bread and peeled my hard boiled egg. My classmates laughed at this, but deep down they were jealous that I had a "Super Mom." She was my cub scout den mother, signed me up for every sport, took me to every lesson, and attended every game. I once had to sit for hours while my sister Gail tried out for the Dallas Summer Musicals. Even as a kid I thought I would just kill myself.

I never thought about the fact that my mom was patiently sitting there all day without complaining. Most of us know of her commitment to all the holidays. As the family grew, there were 85 people to get Christmas presents for. This process started in the summer and she was on a first name bases with the employees at the UPS store. As I think about it, it wasn't the holiday that was the real end —the holiday was an excuse to give to others.

Like all families ours is imperfect. But many of us try to serve Jesus in our lives directly or indirectly because of my mom's example of faith and commitment to her church. She taught all of us to do our best in all of our endeavors. And yet when we messed up, we were accepted and loved... and even defended. Our parents struggled in the early years of their marriage, but they hung in there, and so she passed down to her children to stay committed to their marriages.

One trait she definitely did not pass down to me was her "cuteness." Even her names were cute— "Bunka", "Nana," and "Memaw." She had many cute expressions. When asked a hard question she would say, "Well, let me stop and think." If I was driving with her in the car, I would pull over and say, "OK, now think," to which she would reply, "I never heard of such a thing." If she was trying to get me to take a picture with her camera, she would say, "Poke the big one." Her headaches were always "splitting headaches" And there was the dance she would do when we ate our cream of wheat, singing, "Whoopsy doopsy doodle doo!" For her 87th birthday party, my son Luke commented on her cuteness when she came to watch him in a bike race. He said "There were many people in the crowd who knew me, but I could tell none were as happy and proud for me as Nana was." He then added, "This is the essence of Nana's cuteness." How can someone who draws their truest happiness by seeing the success and happiness others not be cute?

I've been thinking about whether Virginia, my mom, was the matriarch of our family. It's easy to say yes but when I think of a matriarch I think of someone with a dominant personality.

I believe that title goes to my grandmother, GiGi. Mother wasn't the matriarch of our family— she was the soul of our family. When she passed away, so did much of our family's soul. But we who remain behind have the seed of her soul in each of us. my sister Nancy said we are starting a new era in our family. It is up to each of us to water that seed by keeping our faith and our commitments, by always doing our best, and above all, by keeping family as a big priority. Let's call or drop each other a line, remember each other at holidays, and have family reunions.

The apostle Paul wrote these verses which epitomizes what Virginia stood for: "Do nothing out of selfish ambition or vain conceit, but in humility consider others better than yourselves. Each of you should look not only to your own interests, but also to the interest of others." I am grateful the poor quality of life she endured for the last four months is over.

And I am quite confident she is dancing in heaven right now, singing, "Whoopsy, doopsy, doodle, doo!"

VIRGINIA HIGLEY PENNINGTON

A final note about Patriotism: When we look at people serving their country there are many levels. Some give their life, some fight in wars and survive injury, some fight but don't get injured. Many serve behind the front lines and some serve by what they do to make our country a better place to live. What ever you are called to do, be your best and serve in the best way you can.

CREDITS:

Photos from Virginia (Ginny) Adam Higley's Scrap Books
Readers Digest Life In The Forties
"Remember When..." Booklets 1941, 1943, 1945"
Photo of Bob by Kueka Kaddox
Photo of Nile Kinnick Book On Nile Kinick
Story of Nile Kinnick Book On Nile Kinick
Flight Class Photo 160-C Navy Year Book
Navy Photo of Ensign Robert Higley in Uniform
Navy Photo of Ranger Aircraft Carrier Kansas City Star News Paper
Navy History of Ranger
UNITED STATES AT WAR ! JAPS BOMB OUR BASES The
DesMoines Register Dec.8,1941
Wedding photo Ginny Strauss Payton Photo
Navy Photo
Navy Flier Takes A Bride Kansas City Star News Paper
Robert Higley's Log Book March 1,1941- November 11,1941
WWII lustrated Encyclopedia of Aircraft Carriers and Naval AircraftH
History WW II Silver Star Enhanced Research Library
Signal Man Ernest L. Crochet Journal from on the Ranger
Operation Torch, EYEWITNESS TO WORLD WAR II NEIL KAGAN,
STEPHEN G. HYSLOP
NATIONAL GEOGRAPHIC
The American Heritage Picture History of World War II by C. L.
Sulzberger
THE WALDORF-ASTORIA POST CARD
Bunker Hill U.S. Navy History and Photos
ADD TO A PROUD NAME Article, Kansas City Star
The U.S.S. BUNKER HILL NOVEMBER 1943- NOVEMBER 1944
Yearbook record of a carrier's combat action against the Axis Nations
in the Pacific Published by and for the personnel of the U.S.S. Bunker
Hill At Sea 1944.

RABUAL Bunker Hill Annual, Ultimate Collections WORLD WAR
II DVD HISTORY COLLECTION
Letters from The Navy, friends and family
USS Bunker Hill story and photo after Kamikazes hit it near Okinawa,

National Archives Identifier Photographic File of the Department of the Navy, 1943-1958 Record Group 80'
National Archives taken May 11,1945

Lt Robert Higley Photo, Navy Photo
Flying Cross Description, article in magazine kept in scrap book that did articles on war medals each publication.
SON MISSING IN PACIFIC article, Kansas City Star Newspaper.
Photos of Bob and Ginny's girls and Ginny with girls, Strauss Payton Photography
Photos of Legacy Families by James Grabau and John Wasserburger

Editors: A special thanks to my daughter Alison and son Ryan for suggestions and corrections. I also want to thank Dr. Susanne Caswell for reading, corrections and suggestions as well as my wife Nancy for her patience and help.

Lightning Source UK Ltd.
Milton Keynes UK
UKHW040016010820
367482UK00001BA/170